SPEAKING
Of
Success

INSIGHT PUBLISHING
SEVIERVILLE, TENNESSEE

SPEAKING
Of
Success

Disclaimer: This book is a compilation of ideas from numerous experts who have each contributed a chapter. As such, the views expressed in each chapter are of those who were interviewed and not necessarily of the interviewer or Insight Publishing.

Published by Insight Publishing Company
P.O. Box 4189
Sevierville, Tennessee 37864

10 9 8 7 6 5 4 3 2

Printed in the United States of America

ISBN: 978-1-60013-096-8

Table of Contents

A Message from the Publisher

When we decided to do a series of books on success, we searched long and hard to find just the right combination of authors who were not only a success in business but were successful in their personal life as well.

The authors we found had personal stories to tell that revealed their inner values—values that contributed to the achievements they have made and the positive influence they have on others. These authors are people whom others revere as persons of integrity. They are winners.

Everyone wants to be a winner. I have never met anyone who wants to be a loser. And I'm sure you haven't either. That's why we found some of the best motivational/inspirational speakers and authors in the country to contribute to this series. Some of these men and women are household names. Others are rising stars. All of them have achieved the kind of success all of us want—the kind that sparks enthusiasm in others and leaves an indelible, positive impression.

The road to success is one of hard work and persistence. *Speaking of Success* can help you unlock your potential and inspire you to realize the many possibilities awaiting you as you learn how to remove any mental blocks you might have to the success you deserve.

If you're already well on your way down the success highway, the stories and experiences of these authors will encourage you, inform you, and I guarantee that you will learn something.

It is with great pride that we Insight Publishing present this series, *Speaking of Success.* We think you will discover that you will find something new each time you read through these books.

The chapters in this series are real page-turners, so get ready to be inspired. Get ready to be delighted. Get ready to learn. And remember, *you* are the author of your own success journey. Others can shine a light on the path but you must do the walking.

Interviews conducted by:
David E. Wright
President, International Speakers Network

Chapter 1

DARIN EICH

David Wright (Wright)

Today we're talking with Darin Eich. Darin helps people learn how to become themselves, find and live their strengths, and become more innovative people and leaders. He is a professional speaker, consultant, educator, facilitator, motivator, and brainstormer. He is founder of CollegeMotivation.com and is currently the Chief Operating Officer of BrainReactions, a professional brainstorming and innovation services company. Darin does a wide variety of very cool projects ranging from speaking to helping institutions develop leadership programs and retreats to facilitating professional brainstorm innovation sessions for some of the most innovative Fortune 500 corporations.

Darin has been a graduate student at the College of William and Mary, the University of Maryland, and is currently finishing his PhD at the University of Wisconsin. Darin has authored a variety of leadership development publications and is finishing his leadership development doctoral dissertation detailing his research-based theory of high quality leadership programs.

Darin, welcome to *Speaking of Success.*

Darin Eich (Eich)

Thank you so much, David. I really appreciate being a part of this project.

Wright

So how have you found success in your own life?

Eich

Success is a really a fascinating thing for me to discover because it's something I've taken a specific and disciplined look at. When I recall my high school years, I was a mediocre, average person who was not really experiencing a lot of success in much of anything. There came a time later in life when I started to study success and what it means. I don't think many people study success. They study other things such as math, biology, chemistry, political science, etc., but really studying success was the turning point for me in my own life. I started finding myself successful in many areas just by studying them. What really mattered was that I approached success as a discipline—to look at success in a focused way.

What I tried to do was to look at theory and bring that theory into practice. For example, I was reading many books on success, listening to a lot of motivational tapes, and seeing what those speakers had to say about success. It was like a course I outlined for myself on "How to Be Successful 101." I took that and figured out how I could apply it in my own life and how could I do some of the things these successful people were suggesting in order to also be successful. By doing that, I began to experience more success in my own life.

Essentially I took a systems approach to living my life—I built a success system and a strategy around how to achieve success. When you build a system, things change. You start to notice things more and you start to be more deliberate in your actions. The biggest change for me was that my perspective of failure started to change. Previously, failures were disappointments, but when I began to see my life as a success system, those failures took on new meaning. Most failures are very valuable because now all of a sudden they become new "learnings." They are opportunities for development, ways you can learn about yourself, and ways you can learn to improve your system.

I also went back to the basics to find success by observing kindergartners. When I observed them, I thought kindergartners were some of the most successful people I'd ever seen. If you go into a kindergarten classroom and ask the students there, "How many of you can sing? How many of you can dance? How many of you can draw?" they will all jump up and down ready to sing and dance and draw. If you ask those same questions to adults in companies and organizations today, grown-ups are not as eager to do that. Kindergartners had something I really wanted—a willingness to get out there and take risks. I thought that would be success for me—to be a bit like a kindergartner. To do that I had to take an inner journey to figure out who I am.

Wright

How do you figure out who you are and also what you should be doing?

Eich

Figuring out who you are is very challenging but it is vital. It takes some serious effort. I think there are many ways to do it such as determining what your personality is, what your values are, and identifying and clarifying your strengths. There are assessments or surveys you can take. Sometimes they're free online and sometimes they are part of a workshop. They were very handy in helping me to figure out some different pieces of myself and to validate what I may think in a more formal way. You can also talk with different people you know—people you can trust—such as family members, friends, and people you work with. You can get insights from them about who you are by figuring out how they perceive you—how they think you tick.

You also need to sit down and do some serious reflection on some key questions that can help you figure out who you are and what your life is about. I've identified a few questions that get to the heart of the issue. I like a quote from Carl Rogers who said, "What I am is good enough if I can just be it." Something else you hear often is, "Just be yourself." It's wise advice and it's simple advice, but it is surprisingly difficult to do. It's hard to be yourself if you don't know who you are and you need to figure out who you are to begin with.

A topic I've reflected on, and it's a topic I've encouraged others to reflect on when I do workshops and seminars, is what people value. What are your core values? Another question I ask is what are your strengths—what are your skills and talents? I also ask those in my audiences to reflect on what the greatest experiences of their life have been. You need to look back on your life and take assessment of those greatest experiences and write about them a bit. I also think that how you are different from your peers really matters. It's important to take a look at your family members, friends, and people you work with and then pinpoint how you are different from them and what makes you unique.

A bigger picture question is about the gifts you have to offer. We all have some special abilities as individuals and we need to find out what those gifts are and how we can use them to enrich others' lives. Ultimately, what kind of person do you want to be? What do you want the future to be like for you? Being able to think about and answer these questions is important in helping you figure out who you are and what you should be doing with you life.

One conclusion I came up with when I answered these questions for myself is how do I find out ultimately what I should be doing in my life—my career? After the questions of who I am were answered, the kind of career I should have resided at the intersection of my values, my interests, my strengths, and those greatest experiences.

In answering those questions you will know what you can give to the world, what you're interested in giving, and what you're good at giving. You can articulate your own story and in doing so you'll find out a lot about yourself.

Wright

How did you figure it out for yourself?

Eich

It's a beautiful thing when you can begin to figure it out for yourself. I think everyone is always figuring it out and I think that's what makes this fun. As I see it, success is half art and half science—you can learn some things that are working for a lot of people but you also need to creatively make sense of it for yourself.

There are a lot of different ways you can gain insight. For example, one way I did it was by noticing what my daydreams or sleep dreams were. Last week I had this amazing dream where I was put on the spot to give a speech and lead small groups of people in team development activities. I was really challenged to do that. In this dream I felt a lot of joy about doing it, which told me something—I realized I liked to work in those environments. I like to be spontaneous. I like to be creative on the spot. I like to work with people and help them develop as individuals and as a team.

Another tip I have for figuring out for yourself who you are and what you're interested in is take a look at your library record. Look at the books you've checked out. Take a look at the audio tapes you've listened to. I found I was checking out books written by Leo Buscaglia, Zig Ziglar, Les Brown—motivational books and tapes. I had turned my car into a listening library because I was listening to these tapes so much. I realized personal development was something I really was passionate about and deeply interested in. I love talking about success and reading about leadership and ideas. This made me realize that I really gravitate toward those fundamental things in life.

Reflect on the experiences you've had. That will make a difference in figuring out who you are. For example, I thought about the greatest experiences in my life. A lot of them revolved around being with college students in a university environment. It would also involve being in something like a leadership retreat where we go somewhere as a group and develop as people and challenge ourselves and develop friendships fast. There's just an energetic atmosphere around meeting new people. I was first exposed to an experience like this when I was a sophomore in college and I've tried to replicate those experiences in my life. I am also energized when I am a part of brainstorming sessions where I'm both giving ideas and facilitating the generation of ideas from others. Luckily, I get to do this for a living and on a weekly basis. I always leave these session fulfilled because I used my strengths.

Those kinds of experiences really stand out for me as being the greatest experiences of my life. This can help you figure out what you should be doing in the future too. I thought, "I really like these personal development books and I like leadership retreats. What if I could do that for a living? What if I could create my own leadership development experience and personal development experience for people?"

When you assess your own life experiences and keep experiencing new things, you will gain insight to who you are and what your strengths are.

Wright

How do you leverage your strengths?

Eich

Yes, a key opportunity for success is leveraging your strengths. We all have different skill sets. I'm amazed at how different people are.

There are some things that others are interested in that I have no interest in at all. There are things I'm very interested in that other people couldn't care less about. Our differences present an opportunity to collaborate on our strengths with others—to come together and create some pretty amazing things.

When you leverage your strengths you first need to find out how you can use them. I've done a lot of research on my own strengths and on who I am. There are some books written about a new branch of psychology called "positive psychology." It's a research based way of looking at your own personal development. Some of the best books I'd recommend are: *Flow: The Psychology of Optimal Experience* by Mihaly Csikszentmihalyi, *Authentic Happiness,* by Dr. Martin Seligman (founder of positive psychology), and *Now Discover Your Strengths* by Marcus Buckingham and Donald O. Clifton. These books are very helpful in helping you get a good look at who you are and what your strengths are. There are also assessments available with them. One assessment I took online showed me what my signature strengths were.

I think it really matters to get specific about your strengths. You may find that one of your strengths is communicating with people. Then get more specific with that. What is it about communicating with people that you are exceptionally good at? It could be that your real strength is communicating with people in groups but perhaps you're not as good communicating with people one-on-one. Maybe you are good at communicating with people using e-mail but not as good at talking with people on the phone. Maybe you're good at meeting with people in person.

Once you get into general strengths then it helps to get more and more specific. When you do that you can leverage your strengths a little bit more.

I also look for opportunities to innovate how I operate and focus on those strengths. For example, I may have something completely new that I'm working on such as a new conference. I consider what my strengths are and how I can apply them in a new and different way. It's important to continually think about being able to come up with creative new ways to use your strengths so that you don't get stuck in a rut doing the same thing over and over again.

Finally, I think success isn't a one-man job—it's definitely a many person job. On the other side of the strengths coin is weakness. Previously, a major focus of personal development was to identify your weaknesses and improve them rather than embrace your strengths and grow from your strengths. I think there are still opportunities in weaknesses, especially if there are some weaknesses that are pretty glaring. I've come to a point in my life where I've realized my weak points and they're probably not going to change very much. I look for opportunities to collaborate with people who have strengths where I have weaknesses. For example, we have a company that does professional brainstorming. There is a lot more involved with this besides generating ideas. I'm not good with computer technology and creating Web applications. I'm also not that great at making numerous connections with people right away but I have a business partner and others with whom I work who are amazing at doing those things. So there are strengths I bring to the table and strengths they bring to the table that offset my weaknesses. Together we can do some amazing things. I can come up with a lot of good ideas in a session but I can't take those ideas to the next level in drawing what they could look like. That's why we collaborate with some remarkable artists who can do what I cannot.

Wright

How do you innovate yourself?

Eich

It all starts with learning and development. Sometimes people stop changing, growing, and innovating themselves. I think organizations are a lot better at innovating than individual people are. A story you hear a lot is about a classic biology experiment with a frog. If you put the frog in hot water he'll jump out—he sees a real reason to change and jump out. But if you take that same frog and put him in a pot of water at room temperature, he will sit there and enjoy the water. If you turn the heat up the frog will sooner or later boil to death because he didn't perceive the gradual change—change crept up on the frog slowly. I've seen that happen in many places. I fight that with myself too. People stop changing and growing and innovating. They stop seeking to learn and get better. It's important to fight that. The key is to take control of your own learning and seek opportunities to innovate yourself.

Another important element of this is learning how to learn. People learn in different ways. Some people learn by experiencing something, others do best by sitting back and listening. Others like to apply what they've learned personally to something they're doing. There are all sorts of different learning styles.

Do you learn best by reading a book by yourself or do you learn best by talking about it with others? Figure out your learning style and that is the place where you go to innovate yourself. Again, there are a number of great books, online assessments, and Web sites you can search to help you identify your learning style.

You can learn from almost anything. Some of my greatest teachers have been friends' dogs. I learn a lot about how to treat people by watching dogs. Dogs know how to do it. Dogs are man's best friend for a reason. You can see some amazing loyalty, interpersonal relations, and love demonstrated in what a dog does. So learning happens everywhere, you just have to keep your eyes open and be open to learning.

After you start to learn and see yourself and the world in new and more real ways, then the tough part comes, which means changing. If you're going to innovate yourself you're going to constantly change, you're going to constantly get better. You'll perhaps do something new or do something different. That's why changing is a tough thing for people. Sometimes we can get into ruts and be closed to learning new things. Sometimes we can be hesitant to take action on new ideas. We need to develop the courage to innovate. I think the first thing to do is generate ideas about what you want to innovate. Ideas are really crucial for innovating.

Wright

Why do ideas matter so much?

Eich

The greatest kinds of transformations and innovations in our society start from ideas. Our company brings together very innovative college students and younger people to come up with ideas for major Fortune 500 companies. We've done many projects for companies like P&G and even the United Nations. We think that college students have a very strong ability to come up with many creative ideas. Think of some of the greatest recent innovations: Google was started by two graduate students at Stanford University. Federal Express was developed by a college student in a course project. Michael Dell, founder and chairman of Dell Inc., founded the company as PCs Limited with just $1000, in his dorm room while still a student at the University of Texas at Austin in 1984. Bill Gates dropped out of Harvard during his third year to pursue a career in software development and from that came the Microsoft Corporation. The list goes on and on. Facebook, a social networking service, is a very current innovative business developed by a Harvard college student, Mark Zukerberg. College students have an ability to come up with some pretty amazing ideas that can lead to innovations in our society.

We need to go back to that time in our lives when we were less constrained and more open to coming up with ideas. Ideas can serve as motivation as well. When we have a cool idea in our life, it gets us excited. If you have a really good idea and a very clear vision on it, that is motivating. It is motivating for you to move it forward.

Wright

How does one generate ideas?

Eich

We've had a lot of success in being able to generate a great quantity and quality of ideas in brainstorming sessions. In our sessions that last between two and three hours, we usually come up with over 500 ideas. One time we generated over 1,000 ideas. We've done that the same way I'm talking about success—by developing a system. You figure out how to do it, you study it, and then you create a system to make it happen. I think the key here for generating ideas is to do it deliberately.

Currently, I'm helping a university in Michigan develop a system of activities for students to develop ideas for a business or a product they'd like to create. I was also in Tokyo earlier this year meeting with professors at universities. They said they know how to take those ideas and make them real and make them happen but we need help in coming up with ideas in the first place. So there is certainly a great interest in generating ideas, because that is where everything starts. And I think you can do it deliberately. I think you can take a systematic approach to it.

One thing that has been key for us in generating great ideas, first of all, is coming up with good questions for what we want ideas to be about. So that's the first step—the questions. After that, the key that a lot of people overlook is the need to come up with many, many alternatives and a lot of different ideas. Typically, when I work with people, I ask them to come up with at least one hundred ideas for their project. That's a lot of ideas and that's what a lot people and a lot of organizations don't do—they stop after they gather just a few ideas. But you need to formulate many, many ideas. If you capture a lot of ideas then you can make a large list that you can analyze. If you come up with a hundred ideas, odds are there are going to be one or two that are very good. The odds will be less if you only come up with five ideas. If you come up with a hundred ideas you might be able to identify some themes among those ideas when looking at the whole idea list. You might be able to combine a few different ideas together to make an even better idea. So you need to have a very large quantity of ideas first. Quantity will lead to quality.

There are some different tools and techniques you can use to come up with ideas. You can put yourself in other people's shoes, you can break down the question into all kinds of different attributes, you can create mind maps, which are visual representations of a concept, and then see how that concept branches out into new concepts. For instance, you could read this book, *Speaking of Success,* and mind map your own success system based on the best of what each author says. You can read the whole book and then create a mind map of what success means you. You can do this by putting the word "success" in the middle of a piece of paper and circle it and then create spokes from the circle and put what success means to you at the end of each spoke. Creating a mind map has been a valuable tool for me. You can create a mind map of your success system or what success means to you while reading this book. You can integrate all of the different perspectives from people who have thought a lot about this topic and apply it to your own life strategically through this mind map picture you create.

Doing idea generating is an important first project. Whatever the question is that you want to answer with the idea generation process, go about answering it deliberately. Come up with the list and then analyze it. Idea generating is not something you want to do completely on your own. There are some folks you may know who are really creative, who have a good capacity for coming up with ideas. That's the strengths-based approach again. Why not ask them for some ideas on what you're doing? That would be key to being able to collaborate for the purpose of coming up with ideas.

Another guideline here is now that you're coming up with a large quantity of ideas, realize that you're only doing idea generating, you're not doing idea analysis—you're not judging any of the ideas—you're just getting a huge list of alternatives out there. The analysis and judgment happens later. Another problem people have is every time they come up with an idea their mind goes into judging that idea and finding out reasons the idea won't work.

Idea generating, much like success, comes down to finding your own style and being able to do it deliberately and purposefully.

Wright

How do you take action?

Eich

When you've whittled down all the ideas to one good concept, what do you do next? That's a huge concern because too many people get stuck right at that point. They've got the idea but they're not taking action on it.

The first thing to help you take action is that the idea has to be developed and it has to be great, exciting, and motivating. The idea should give you a compelling vision of the future. I don't think a lot of ideas get to that place where they motivate people. Being able to formulate that vision from the idea and making sure it's a good one will motivate you to take action on it.

Continually doing systems learning is important. When you're doing a systems learning approach, the key is learning to create a system. So your first action is to anticipate that you'll fail. Anytime we do something the first time, we aren't great at it but the opportunity is there to learn from that first action. So the first time or second or third time you take action your expectations aren't for a huge success. You'll be testing things out so you're doing some things to improve and create a system.

We all have our own style for taking action. Personally I know that I'm always better with people than I am by myself, so I'll find a collaborator and do it with someone else. I also need a lot of structure, so I'll build myself a structure or I'll break down a huge project into tiny pieces to work on for perhaps ten minutes a day. Discover your own action style and break your project down into small pieces.

Ultimately, taking that first action, learning from that, and then incorporating it all into your system for success will help you take action and make those actions continually better. When you view it as a system and recognize that failure is an expected part of that system, it is easier to develop courage to act. You can find places and people to "test" your first actions and get those failures out of the way for learning before doing the really important things.

Wright

Considering what you have said here, what have you learned about success?

Eich

The first thing I've learned about success is that I always need to be focused on learning about it. I don't think I can ever stop. I think that's when "rust" will start to accumulate in my mind—when I lose that willingness to learn.

When I started my journey in college learning about success I always focused on how to be successful. Now I'm thinking about it differently. I consider specifically: success for what? I study leadership and am developing a theory of high quality of leadership development programs for my dissertation. The question I keep coming back to is leadership for what? Why do we want to be successful? Why do we want to be better leaders and engage in this process called leadership? Success for what? Innovation for what? Ideas for what? Why? Many people want to earn money. What do they want to earn money specifically for? What is the purpose here? I think those questions are the next step to think about.

For me, a lot of it should be centered on the principle of love. Is what I'm trying to do here a loving thing? Is it helping others? If not then I probably shouldn't be doing it. I should focus on things I can do to make a positive contribution to my society.

Considering all these questions is where I'm going next in learning about success—success for what?

I always thought I was successful because I had these excellent professional achievements and a wonderful career. I was grounded when I realized that success wasn't just a career—there are a lot of different aspects to life other than a career. There is also family and friends and health and spirit. Some people may be very focused and successful in some areas but less so in others. Being able to look at one's life more holistically and see the big picture really matters as well.

You can also be successful by focusing on the foundations—on the basics. You can be successful by staying out of trouble. Some people make some very bad decisions that throw them. You need to take positive risks that don't have significant negative consequences. Be good to others; if you're good to others then they will be good to you. Live with integrity. Experience different things, places, and people. I think we can understand a lot more about who we are and how we can be successful and innovate ourselves when we consider who we are in relation to other people and places. Go travel somewhere else. Go meet people who are very different from you. Try some different roles because that will help you articulate who you are.

Remaining open and willing to change is a part of learning too. You will incorporate change into your life by innovating and knowing that you can continually improve as a person and do things better.

One big thing I've learned about success is I think it happens in moments. I think if you're successful only 1 percent of the time, you can be a really successful person—if you're successful in those right moments. There are critical moments that come up during everyday life that are important. Maybe it's that job interview or it could be that speech or it could be that interaction with a loved one or it could be something that doesn't happen often, but it's really important. If you can claim those moments and master those moments, they will contribute to your success. You really want to perform at your peak during those critical moments.

Wright

How do you transform into your best?

Eich

I think we all have a recipe for how we can transform into our best. I think about Superman. He was a mild-mannered reporter named Clark Kent but when he would go into the phone booth he would transform into Superman. We need to figure out what our "phone booth" is to be super men and women. How can we transform and what can we do to make us our best in a quick instant?

There are a number of different recipes for that transformation you can make; you just need to figure out your own recipe. One thing that is important for me is to control the negative self-talk that happens in my mind. For example, if I have an idea and I'm judging it or if I want to do something and my mind is trying to talk myself out of it, I need to stop that. The first step is to take a look at the chatter that is going on in the mind and start talking yourself into it instead of talking yourself out of it. You always run into people who have an idea and when you ask what they did with it they'll say they talked themselves out of it. Rarely do you hear people say they talked themselves into it. Replace the negative in your mind with positive. Write down what your mind is telling you and if it's negative and irrational, replace it with something positive that affirms who you are and what you can do.

I've gone so far as to create a personal anthem. It's a short poem that I'll say to myself to get pumped up and motivated. I'll say, "I'm motivated and perspirated, divinely inspired and desired; blood, sweat, teared, feared; talent given and driven. I'm calm, cool, collected, and respected. I'm a time bomb about to explode. I feel like a pregnant woman ready to give birth and a starving man waiting to eat. I'm back and on the attack, ready, willing, and able. I'm ready." This saying will motivate me—it's my trigger. So whenever I say that to myself I can't help but transform into a better self. (Plus saying that out loud is a lot of fun!)

Ask yourself what other pieces of a recipe for yourself can you make? Can you visualize yourself being successful in what you're doing? If there is a friend you have who really motivates you; can you call that friend before you go at it and do that important thing you're going to do? What makes you feel good? Is it looking at old photos or old videos of you at your best? Is it a shirt that you wore during some important successful moment in the past? Find all those things that you can to trigger yourself to being at your best and identify that recipe to go forward from there.

Wright

What an interesting conversation, Darin. I've learned a lot here today. You certainly are disciplined and I've never heard success spoken about in such a disciplined way.

Today we've been talking with Darin Eich. Darin helps people learn how to find their strengths and become more innovative people. He is a professional speaker, consultant, educator, facilitator, motivator, and brainstormer. He is founder of CollegeMotivation.com and is currently the Chief Operating Officer of BrainReactions.

Darin, thank you so much for being with us today on *Speaking of Success.*

About the Author

DARIN EICH is the Chief Operating Officer of BrainReactions, a professional brainstorming and innovation services company. BrainReactions specializes in "outside innovation" and selects and trains highly creative people to brainstorm new ideas for other organizations. In addition to this, Darin is a professional speaker, trainer, consultant, educator, facilitator, motivator, and brainstormer. His passion involves helping people to learn how to become themselves, find and live their strengths, and become more innovative people and leaders. Professionally, Darin does a wide variety of projects ranging from speaking to helping institutions develop leadership programs and retreats to facilitating professional brainstorm innovation sessions for some of the most innovative Fortune 500 corporations.

Darin has been a graduate student at the College of William and Mary, University of Maryland, and is currently finishing his Phd at the University of Wisconsin in Madison. Darin has authored a variety of innovation and leadership development publications and is finishing his leadership development doctoral dissertation detailing his research based theory of high quality leadership programs. Darin encourages you to drop him an e-mail. For more of Darin's writing you can visit his blog at InnovateYourself.com.

Darin Eich
BrainReactions
520 University Ave., Suite 150
Madison, WI 53703
Phone: 757.869.6993
E-mail: darin.eich@brainreactions.com
www.brainreactions.com
www.collegemotivation.com
www.innovateyourself.com
www.brainreactions.net

Chapter 2

DR. KEN BLANCHARD

THE INTERVIEW

David E. Wright (Wright)

Few people have created a positive impact on the day-to-day management of people and companies more than Dr. Kenneth Blanchard, who is known around the world simply as Ken, a prominent, gregarious, sought-after author, speaker, and business consultant. Ken is universally characterized by friends, colleagues, and clients as one of the most insightful, powerful, and compassionate men in business today. Ken's impact as a writer is far-reaching. His phenomenal best-selling book, *The One Minute Manager®*, co-authored with Spencer Johnson, has sold more than thirteen million copies worldwide and has been translated into more than twenty-five languages. Ken is Chairman and Chief Spiritual Officer of the Ken Blanchard Companies. The organization's focus is to energize organizations around the world with customized training in bottom line business strategies based on the simple, yet powerful principles inspired by Ken's best-selling books.

Dr. Blanchard, welcome to *Speaking of Success*!

Dr. Ken Blanchard (Blanchard)
Well, it's nice to talk to you, David. It's good to be here.

Wright
I must tell you that preparing for your interview took quite a bit more time than usual. The scope of your life's work and your business, the Ken Blanchard Companies, would make for a dozen fascinating interviews. Before we dive into the specifics of some of your projects and strategies, will you give our readers a brief synopsis of your life—how you came to be the Ken Blanchard we all know and respect?

Blanchard
Well, I'll tell you, David, I think life is what you do when you are planning on doing something else. I think that was John Lennon's line. I never intended to do what I have been doing. In fact, all my professors in college told me that I couldn't write. I wanted to do college work, which I did, and they said, "You had better be an administrator." So I decided I was going to be a Dean of Students. I got provisionally accepted into my master's degree program and then provisionally accepted at Cornell, because I never could take any of those standardized tests.

I took the college boards four times and finally got 502 in English. I don't have a test-taking mind. I ended up in a university in Athens, Ohio, in 1966 as an Administrative Assistant to the Dean of the Business School. When I got there he said, "Ken, I want you to teach a course. I want all my deans to teach." I had never thought about teaching because they said I couldn't write, and teachers had to publish. He put me in the manager's department.

I've taken enough bad courses in my day and I wasn't going to teach one. I really prepared and had a wonderful time with the students. I was chosen as one of the top ten teachers on the campus coming out of the chute!

I just had a marvelous time. A colleague by the name of Paul Hersey was chairman of the management department. He wasn't very friendly to me initially because the Dean had led me into his department, but I heard he was a great teacher. He taught organizational behavior and leadership. So I said, "Can I sit in on your course next semester?"

"Nobody audits my courses," he said. "If you want to take it for credit, you're welcome."

I couldn't believe it. I had a doctoral degree and he wanted me to take his course for credit, so I signed up.

The registrar didn't know what to do with me because I already had a doctorate, but I wrote the papers and took the course, and it was great.

In June 1967, Hersey came into my office and said, "Ken, I've been teaching in this field for ten years. I think I'm better than anybody, but I can't write. I'm a nervous wreck, and I'd love to write a textbook with somebody. Would you write one with me?"

I said, "We ought to be a great team. You can't write and I'm not supposed to be able to, so let's do it!"

Thus began this great career of writing and teaching. We wrote a textbook called *Management of Organizational Behavior: Utilizing Human Resources*. It came out in its eighth edition October 3, 2000 and the nineth edition will be out June 15, 2007. It has sold more than any other textbook in that area over the years. It's been over forty years since that book came out.

I quit my administrative job, became a professor, and ended up working my way up the ranks. I got a sabbatical leave and went to California for one year twenty-five years ago. I ended up meeting Spencer Johnson at a cocktail party. He wrote children's books—a wonderful series called *Value Tales for Kids including.* He also wrote *The Value of Courage: The Story of Jackie Robinson and The Value of Believing In Yourself: The Story Louis Pasteur.*

My wife, Margie, met him first and said, "You guys ought to write a children's book for managers because they won't read anything else." That was my introduction to Spencer. So, *The One Minute Manager* was really a kid's book for big people. That is a long way from saying that my career was well planned.

Wright

Ken, what and/or who were your early influences in the areas of business, leadership and success? In other words, who shaped you in your early years?

Blanchard

My father had a great impact on me. He was retired as an admiral in the Navy and had a wonderful philosophy. I remember when I was elected as president of the seventh grade, and I came home all pumped up. My father said, "Son, it's great that you're the president of the seventh grade, but now that you have that leadership position, don't ever use it." He said, "Great leaders are followed because people respect them and like them, not because they have power." That was a wonderful lesson for me early on. He was just a great model for me. I got a lot from him.

Then I had this wonderful opportunity in the mid 1980s to write a book with Norman Vincent Peale. He wrote *The Power of Positive Thinking*. I met him when he was eighty-six years old and we were asked to write a book on ethics together, *The Power of Ethical Management: Integrity Pays, You Don't Have to Cheat to Win*. It didn't matter what we were writing together, I learned so much from him, and he just built from the positive things I learned from my mother.

My mother said that when I was born I laughed before I cried, I danced before I walked, and I smiled before I frowned. So that, as well as Norman Vincent Peale, really impacted me as I focused on what I could do to train leaders. How do you make them positive? How do you make them realize that it's not about them, it's about who they are serving. It's not about their position, it's about what they can do to help other people win.

So, I'd say my mother and father, then Norman Vincent Peale, all had a tremendous impact on me.

Wright

I can imagine. I read a summary of your undergraduate and graduate degrees. I assumed you studied business administration, marketing management, and related courses. Instead, at Cornell you studied government and philosophy. You received your master's from Colgate in sociology and counseling and your PhD from Cornell in educational administration and leadership. Why did you choose this course of study? How has it affected your writing and consulting?

Blanchard

Well, again, it wasn't really well planned out. I originally went to Colgate to get a master's degree in education because I was going to be a Dean of Students over men. I had been a government major, and I was a government major because it was the best department at Cornell in the Liberal Arts School. It was exciting. We would study what the people were doing at the league governments. And then, the Philosophy Department was great. I just loved the philosophical arguments. I wasn't a great student in terms of getting grades, but I'm a total learner. I would sit there and listen, and I would really soak it in.

When I went over to Colgate and got in these education courses, they were awful. They were boring. The second week, I was sitting at the bar at the Colgate Inn saying, "I can't believe I've been here two years for this." It's just the way the Lord works—sitting next to me in the bar was a young sociology professor who had just gotten his PhD at Illinois. He was staying at the Inn. I was moaning and groaning about what I was doing, and he said, "Why don't you come and major with me in sociology? It's really exciting."

"I can do that?" I asked.

He said, "Yes."

I knew they would probably let me do whatever I wanted the first week. Suddenly, I switched out of education and went with Warren Ramshaw. He had a tremendous impact on me. He retired some years ago as the leading professor at Colgate in the Arts and Sciences, and got me interested in leadership and organizations. That's why I got a master's in sociology.

The reason I went into educational administration and leadership? It was a doctoral program I could get into because I knew the guy heading up the program. He said, "The greatest thing about Cornell is that you will be in a School of Education. It's not very big, so you don't have to take many education courses, and you can take stuff all over the place."

There was a marvelous man by the name of Don McCarty, who eventually became the Dean of the School of Education, Wisconsin. He had an impact on my life; but I was always just searching around. My mission statement is: to be a loving teacher and example of simple truths that help myself and others to awaken the presence of God in our lives. The reason I mention "God" is that I believe the biggest addiction in the world is the human ego; but I'm really into simple truth. I used to tell people I was trying to get the B.S. out of the behavioral sciences.

Wright

I can't help but think, when you mentioned your father, that he just bottomed lined it for you about leadership.

Blanchard

Yes.

Wright

A man named Paul Myers, in Texas, years and years ago when I went to a conference down there, said, "David, if you think you're a leader and you look around, and no one is following you, you're just out for a walk."

Blanchard

Well, you'd get a kick; I'm just reaching over to pick up a picture of Paul Myers on my desk. He's a good friend, and he's a part of our Center for FaithWalk Leadership where we're trying to challenge and equip people to lead like Jesus. It's non-profit. I tell people I'm not an evangelist because we've got enough trouble with the Christians we have. We don't need any more new ones. But, this is a picture of Paul on top of a mountain. Then there's another picture below that of him under the sea with stingrays. It says, "Attitude is everything. Whether you're on the top of the mountain or the bottom of the sea, true happiness is achieved by accepting God's promises, and by having a biblically positive frame of mind. Your attitude is everything." Isn't that something?

Wright

He's a fine, fine man. He helped me tremendously. In keeping with the theme of our book, *Speaking of Success,* I wanted to get a sense from you about your own success journey. Many people know you best from *The One Minute Manager* books you coauthored with Spencer Johnson. Would you consider these books as a high water mark for you, or have you defined success for yourself in different terms?

Blanchard

Well, you know, *The One Minute Manager* was an absurdly successful book, so quickly that I found I couldn't take credit for it. That was when I really got on my own spiritual journey and started to try to find out what the real meaning of life and success was.

That's been a wonderful journey for me because I think, David, the problem with most people is they think their self-worth is a function of their performance plus the opinion of others. The minute you think that is what your self-worth is, every day your self-worth is up for grabs because your performance is going to fluctuate on a day-to-day basis. People are fickle. Their opinions are going to go up and down. You need to ground your self-worth in the unconditional love that

God has ready for us, and that really grew out of the unbelievable success of *The One Minute Manager.*

When I started to realize where all that came from, that's how I got involved in this ministry that I mentioned. Paul Myers is a part of it. As I started to read the Bible, I realized that everything I've ever written about, or taught, Jesus did. You know, He did it with the twelve incompetent guys He "hired." The only guy with much education was Judas, and he was His only turnover problem.

Wright

Right.

Blanchard

It was a really interesting thing. What I see in people is not only do they think their self-worth is a function of their performance plus the opinion of others, but they measure their success on the amount of accumulation of wealth, on recognition, power, and status. I think those are nice success items. There's nothing wrong with those, as long as you don't define your life by that.

What I think you need to focus on rather than success is what Bob Buford, in his book *Halftime,* calls significance—moving from success to significance. I think the opposite of accumulation of wealth is generosity.

I wrote a book called *The Generosity Factor* with Truett Cathy, who is the founder of Chick-fil-A. He is one of the most generous men I've ever met in my life. I thought we needed to have a model of generosity. It's not only your treasure, but it's your time and talent. Truett and I added *touch* as a fourth one.

The opposite of recognition is service. I think you become an adult when you realize you're here to serve rather than to be served.

Finally, the opposite of power and status is loving relationships. Take Mother Teresa as an example; she couldn't have cared less about recognition, power, and status because she was focused on generosity, service, and loving relationships; but she got all of that earthly stuff. If you focus on the earthly, such as money, recognition, and power, you're never going to get to significance. But if you focus on significance, you'll be amazed at how much success can come your way.

Wright

I spoke with Truett Cathy recently and was impressed by what a down-to-earth, good man he seems to be. When you start talking about him closing on Sunday, all of my friends—when they found out I had talked to him—said, "Boy, he must be a great Christian man, but he's rich and all this." I told them, "Well, to put his faith into perspective, by closing on Sunday it cost him $500 million a year." He lives his faith, doesn't he?

Blanchard

Absolutely, but he still outsells everybody else.

Blanchard

That's right.

Blanchard

According to their January 25, 2007, press release, Chick-fil-A is currently the nation's second-largest quick-service chicken restaurant chain in sales. Its business performance marks the thirty-ninth consecutive year the chain has enjoyed a system-wide sales gain—a streak the company has sustained since opening its first chain restaurant in 1967.

Wright

The simplest market scheme, I told him, tripped me up. I walked by his first Chick-fil-A I had ever seen, and some girl came out with chicken stuck on toothpicks and handed me one; I just grabbed it and ate it, it's history from there on.

Blanchard

Yes, I think so. It's really special. It is so important that people understand generosity, service, and loving relationships because too many people are running around like a bunch of peacocks. You even see pastors who measure their success by how many in are in their congregation; authors by how many books they have sold; businesspeople by what their profit margin is—how good sales are. The reality is that's all well and good, but I think what you need to focus on is the other. I think if business did that more and we got Wall Street off our backs with all the short-term evaluation, we'd be a lot better off.

Wright

Absolutely. There seems to be a clear theme that winds through many of your books that have to do with success in business and organizations—how people are treated by management and how they feel about their value to a company. Is this an accurate observation? If so, can you elaborate on it?

Blanchard

Yes, it's a very accurate observation. See, I think the profit is the applause you get for taking care of your customers and creating a motivating environment for your people. Very often people think that business is only about the bottom line. But no, that happens to be the result of creating raving fan customers, which I've described with Sheldon Bowles in our book, *Raving Fans*. Customers want to brag about you, if you create an environment where people can be gung-ho and committed. You've got to take care of your customers and your people, and then your cash register is going to go ka-ching, and you can make some big bucks.

Wright

I noticed that your professional title with the Ken Blanchard Companies is somewhat unique—Chairman and Chief Spiritual Officer. What does your title mean to you personally and to your company? How does it affect the books you choose to write?

Blanchard

I remember having lunch with Max DuPree one time, the legendary Chairman of Herman Miller, who wrote a wonderful book called *Leadership Is An Art.* "What's your job?" I asked him.

He said, "I basically work in the vision area."

"Well, what do you do?" I asked.

"I'm like a third grade teacher," he replied. "I say our vision and values over, and over, and over again until people get it right, right, right."

I decided from that, I was going to become the Chief Spiritual Officer, which means I would be working in the vision, values, and energy part of our business. I ended up leaving a morning message every day for everybody in our company. We have twenty-eight international offices around the world. I leave a voice mail every morning, and I do three things on that as Chief Spiritual Officer: One, people tell me who we need to pray for. Two, people tell me who we need to praise—

our unsung heroes and people like that. And then three, I leave an inspirational morning message. I really am the cheerleader—the Energizer Bunny—in our company. I'm the reminder of why we're here and what we're trying to do.

We think that our business in the Ken Blanchard Companies is to help people lead at a higher level, and to help individuals and organizations. Our mission statement is to unleash the power and potential of people and organizations for the common good. So if we are going to do that, we've really got to believe in that.

I'm working on getting more Chief Spiritual Officers around the country. I think it's a great title and we should get more of them.

Wright

I had the pleasure of reading one of your releases, *The Leadership Pill*.

Blanchard

Yes.

Wright

I must admit that my first thought was how short the book was. I wondered if I was going to get my money's worth, which by the way, I most certainly did. Many of your books are brief and based on a fictitious story. Most business books in the market today are hundreds of pages in length and are read almost like a textbook.

Will you talk a little bit about why you write these short books, and about the premise of *The Leadership Pill?*

Blanchard

I really developed my relationship with Spencer Johnson when we wrote *The One Minute Manager.* As you know, he wrote, *Who Moved My Cheese*, which was a phenomenal success. He wrote children's books, and is quite a storyteller.

Jesus taught by parables, which were short stories.

My favorite books are, *Jonathan Livingston Seagull* and *The Little Prince.*

Og Mandino, author of seventeen books, was the greatest of them all.

I started writing parables because people can get into the story and learn the contents of the story, and they don't bring their judgmental hats into reading. You write a regular book and they'll say,

"Well, where did you get the research?" They get into that judgmental side. Our books get them emotionally involved and they learn.

The Leadership Pill is a fun story about a pharmaceutical company who thinks that they have discovered the secret to leadership, and they can put the ingredients in a pill. When they announce it, the country goes crazy because everybody knows we need more effective leaders. When they release it, it outsells Viagra. The founders of the company start selling off stock and they call them Pillionaires. But along comes this guy who calls himself "the effective manager," and he challenges them to a no-pill challenge. If they identify two non-performing groups, he'll take on one and let somebody on the pill take another one, and he guarantees he will out-perform that person by the end of the year. They agree, but of course they give him a drug test every week to make sure he's not sneaking pills on the side.

I wrote the book with Marc Muchnick, who is a young guy in his early thirties. We did a major study of what this interesting "Y" generation, the young people of today, want from leaders, and this is a secret blend that this effective manager uses. When you think about it, David, it is really powerful on terms of what people want from a leader.

Number one, they want integrity. A lot of people have talked about that in the past, but these young people will walk if they see people say one thing and do another. A lot of us walk to the bathroom and out into the halls to talk about it. But these people will quit. They don't want somebody to say something and not do it.

The second thing they want is a partnership relationship. They hate superior/subordinate. I mean, what awful terms those are. You know, the "head" of the department and the hired "hands"—you don't even give them a head. "What do you do? I'm in supervision. I see things a lot clearer than these stupid idiots." They want to be treated as partners; if they can get a financial partnership, great. If they can't, they really want a minimum of psychological partnership where they can bring their brains to work and make decisions.

Then finally, they want affirmation. They not only want to be caught doing things right, but they want to be affirmed for who they are. They want to be known as a person, not as a number.

So those are the three ingredients that this effective manager uses. They are wonderful values when you think about them.

Rank-order values for any organization is number one, integrity. In our company we call it ethics. It is our number one value. The number two value is partnership. In our company we call it relationships. Number three is affirmation—being affirmed as a human being. I think that ties into relationships, too. They are wonderful values that can drive behavior in a great way.

Wright

I believe most people in today's business culture would agree that success in business has everything to do with successful leadership. In *The Leadership Pill*, you present a simple but profound premise, that leadership is not something you do to people, it's something you do *with* them. At face value, that seems incredibly obvious. But you must have found in your research and observations that leaders in today's culture do not get this. Would you speak to that issue?

Blanchard

Yes. I think what often happens in this is the human ego. There are too many leaders out there who are self-serving. They're not leaders who have service in mind. They think the sheep are there for the benefit of the shepherd. All the power, money, fame and recognition moves up the hierarchy; they forget that the real action in business is not up the hierarchy; it's in the one-to-one, moment-to-moment interactions that your front line people have with your customers. It's how the phone is answered. It's how problems are dealt with and those kinds of things. If you don't think that you're doing leadership *with* them—rather, you're doing it to them—after a while they won't take care of your customers.

I was at a store once (not Nordstrom's, where I normally would go) and I thought of something I had to share with my wife, Margie. I asked the guy behind the counter in Men's Wear, "May I use your phone?"

He said, "No!"

"You're kidding me," I said. "I can always use the phone at Nordstrom's."

"Look, buddy," he said, "they won't let *me* use the phone here. Why should I let you use the phone?"

That is an example of leadership that's done *to* employees not *with* them. People want a partnership. People want to be involved in a way that really makes a difference.

Wright

Dr. Blanchard, the time has flown by and there are so many more questions I'd like to ask you. In closing, would you mind sharing with our readers some thoughts on success? If you were mentoring a small group of men and women, and one of their central goals was to become successful, what kind of advice would you give them?

Blanchard

Well, I would first of all say, "What are you focused on?" If you are focused on success as being, as I said earlier, accumulation of money, recognition, power, or status, I think you've got the wrong target. What you need to really be focused on is how you can be generous in the use of your time and your talent and your treasure and touch. How can you serve people rather than be served? How can you develop caring, loving relationships with people? My sense is if you will focus on those things, success in the traditional sense will come to you. But if you go out and say, "Man, I'm going to make a fortune, and I'm going to do this," and have that kind of attitude, you might get some of those numbers. I think you become an adult, however, when you realize you are here to give rather than to get. You're here to serve not to be served. I would just say to people, "Life is such a very special occasion. Don't miss it by aiming at a target that bypasses other people, because we're really here to serve each other." So that's what I would share with people.

Wright

Well, what an enlightening conversation, Dr. Blanchard. I really want you to know how much I appreciate all the time you've taken with me for this interview. I know that our readers will learn from this, and I really appreciate your being with us today.

Blanchard

Well, thank you so much, David. I really enjoyed my time with you. You've asked some great questions that made me think, and I hope my answers are helpful to other people because as I say, life is a special occasion.

Wright

Today we have been talking with Dr. Ken Blanchard. He is the author of the phenomenal best selling book, *The One Minute Manager*. The fact that he's the Chief Spiritual Officer of his company should make us all think about how we are leading our companies and leading our families and leading anything, whether it is in church or civic organizations. I know I will.

About The Author

Few people have created more of a positive impact on the day-to-day management of people and companies than Dr. Kenneth Blanchard, who is known around the world simply as "Ken."

When Ken speaks, he speaks from the heart with warmth and humor. His unique gift is to speak to an audience and communicate with each individual as if they were alone and talking one-on-one. He is a polished storyteller with a knack for making the seemingly complex easy to understand.

Ken has been a guest on a number of national television programs, including *Good Morning America* and *The Today Show*. He has been featured in *Time, People, U.S. News & World Report*, and a host of other popular publications.

He earned his bachelor's degree in government and philosophy from Cornell University, his master's degree in sociology and counseling from Colgate University, and his PhD in educational administration and leadership from Cornell University.

Dr. Ken Blanchard
The Ken Blanchard Companies
125 State Place
Escondido, California 92029
Phone: 800.728.6000
Fax: 760.489.8407
www.kenblanchard.com

Chapter 3

LAUREN MACKLER

David Wright (Wright)

Today we're talking with Lauren Mackler. Lauren has helped individuals and organizations turn aspirations into reality and reach the next level of success since 1982. As one of America's leading coaches, Lauren is frequently interviewed by *The Wall Street Journal*, *Boston Globe*, and *Boston Business Journal*, as well as other publications, television, and radio. Her company, Lauren Mackler & Associates (LMA), was recognized as one of the top five coaching firms in the United States and the best in Boston by *Vitals Magazine*.

Fueled by her passion for helping people become the best they can be, Lauren founded LMA in 2001, providing coaching programs, workshops, and consulting services that help clients unleash their greatest potential in their personal lives, careers, relationships, and organizations. Her unique combination of expertise in psychology, business, and career management enables her to work with clients in a variety of areas critical to optimizing personal and professional performance.

Lauren, welcome to *Speaking of Success*.

Lauren Mackler (Mackler)
It's a pleasure to speak with you.

Wright
As I'm sure you know, success can be defined in various ways. How do you define success?

Mackler
Success is subjective and therefore it's defined and experienced by people in different ways. It can be a certain level of income, a large circle of caring and supportive friends, work that is meaningful and rewarding, or a fulfilling partnership or marriage. I define success as being able to activate your greatest potential to produce the circumstances, experiences, relationships, and resources you want to have in your life.

Wright
There are a multitude of books, DVDs, courses, and workshops that provide strategies and tools for achieving greater success. Yet despite the abundance of these resources, why do you think so many people continually find themselves unable to achieve or sustain the level of success to which they aspire?

Mackler
Some of these resources provide tools and strategies for setting goals and developing action plans. Others teach you how to articulate a vision or present the attitudes or behaviors needed for success. They focus on *strategies* for success but typically fail to help people to understand and effectively move through the *barriers* to success. This is why so many people have difficulty translating success strategies into tangible and lasting results.

Many of my coaching clients are highly motivated individuals who come to me after having tried several approaches to achieving success, but have found it difficult to break through to the next level. They have read books, attended seminars, or participated in brief or long-term therapy. However, none of these things produced the results they wanted, leaving them frustrated and in some cases discouraged, thinking that they'd never be able to create the successful life they envisioned.

Wright

What are the barriers to success?

Mackler

The barriers to success are complex, with a multitude of layers. I have found in my twenty-four years of working with clients that the two greatest factors that limit people's success are what I call *limiting core beliefs* and *habitual default behaviors*. While many self-help and therapeutic approaches to achieving success address people's beliefs and behaviors, they more often than not fail to do so at the root level, leaving people frustrated with their inability to move beyond them.

In order to change limiting beliefs and habitual behaviors to ones that foster success, we need to first clearly identify what they are, where they come from, the function they've served in our lives, and the results that they produce.

Wright

Will you define exactly what you mean by "core beliefs" and "habitual behaviors"?

Mackler

Our core beliefs are formed in childhood and are the conclusions we adopt and internalize as truths about ourselves and the world around us. We develop these beliefs in response to the conditioning of our family of origin (the family in which we grew up) as well as to other positive and negative circumstances and experiences to which we are exposed, such as friends, school, and cultural and religious influences. These beliefs are shaped by several factors: the core beliefs passed on to us by our parents (which are directly communicated and indirectly inferred), the experiences and dynamics of our family system, how our parents and other significant role models such as teachers relate to us, and the unique and innate personality traits with which each of us is born.

Our core beliefs are the primary driving forces behind how we respond to or behave in the world—what I refer to as habitual default behaviors. As with our core beliefs, these habitual behaviors are shaped by the conditioning and circumstances to which we were exposed as children. These include: the nature and dynamics of the family system, whether and to what degree the family was a constructive or dysfunctional system, what was allowed or prohibited within the rules and norms of the family system, and the behaviors our parents either reinforced or discouraged through their role modeling and behaviors toward us.

Wright

Will you talk about the characteristics of dysfunctional and constructive family systems, and how they influence our core beliefs and habitual behaviors?

Mackler

Let me start with a foundational overview of family systems and then give you an example to show how the family of origin shapes our beliefs and behaviors.

A family is a microcosm of a larger social system with its own rules and structures. In the psychology field it is often referred to as either an "open" or "closed" system—what I refer to as either "constructive" or "dysfunctional"—with most family systems falling somewhere between the two extremes. The characteristics of a constructive system is one in which the rules and structures are flexible and designed to serve and sustain the system. Our innate capacity to feel and express the full spectrum of human emotions such as anger, joy, and sadness are supported and maintained, and dissimilarities and differences between members are considered normal and respected.

In a dysfunctional system there are either no rules or structures, or rules and structures that are very rigid and inflexible, designed to discourage any opinions or behaviors that threaten the accepted norms of the system. Thinking and behaving in the same way is the rule, with any deviation considered crazy and/or bad. Any emotions or behaviors that threaten the system are suppressed, resulting in the disintegration of the innate wholeness with which we are born (which will vary in severity, depending on the degree to which the system is dysfunctional).

As an example, let's say little two-year-old "Jenny" has her first temper tantrum. In a fit of rage she picks up her toy and throws it against the wall, smashing it to bits. In a system that has predominantly dysfunctional attributes, her parent might react to Jenny's expression of anger through physical punishment, conditioning her to believe that, "If I express anger I'll get hurt." Or it may be through shaming her by saying, "You bad girl, *now* look what you've done," instilling the belief that, "Expressing my anger is bad and I should feel ashamed." The parent might withdraw emotionally and banish

Jenny to her room, invoking the belief that, "If I express anger, I'll lose others' love and they'll abandon me." Another approach might be to rush to Jenny's side and console her, reinforcing the belief that, "Having temper tantrums and acting out gets me love and attention."

Now let's look at how that same example might be played out in a more constructive system. In response to Jenny having her temper tantrum and breaking her toy, her parent might respond by saying, "Jenny, you seem angry; what are you upset about?" This question validates Jenny's feelings and asks what's upsetting her without any judgment. Instead of punishing, shaming, or "rewarding" her for her angry outburst and breaking her toy, her parent teaches her how to express and manage her anger in a constructive manner. She might say, "Well, honey, when we throw our toys against the wall they can get broken. It's better to use words to say what you feel or, if you're very angry, you can punch a pillow so you won't hurt your toys or anyone else." In this example the parent is reinforcing the belief that, "It's normal and safe to express my anger." And by showing Jenny how to discharge her anger by expressing it through words or by punching a pillow, she's teaching her an important life skill of how to express that emotion in a safe and constructive manner.

Wright

Why do parents often end up treating their children as they have been treated—especially people who were the recipients of painful or injurious behaviors by their parents?

Mackler

When left to our own devices (in the absence of personal development work) we tend to automatically replicate that which is familiar to us (what we learned and were exposed to growing up). For this reason we habitually react to our children in the same ways that our parents reacted to us. Even when we vow *never* to treat our children the way our parents treated us, the patterns ingrained in our minds during childhood are so powerful that we inevitably end up replicating them with our spouses, friends, children, and at work. We even replicate them in our relationships with ourselves! People tend to treat themselves as poorly or lovingly as they have been treated by their parents. And, unfortunately, more people originate from a family system that was more dysfunctional than constructive, since family systems tend to mirror the dysfunction that exists in our overall society. As a result, it's not surprising that so many people struggle with issues of self criticism, low self-esteem, and settling for less than what they have the potential to create and experience in their lives.

Wright

The link between a person's level of self-esteem and his or her ability to achieve the success he or she seeks is an interesting point. Will you expand upon this?

Mackler

It's very difficult to create a successful life from an inner emotional base of low self-esteem because you believe you're not worthy or capable of success. People who feel unworthy of success often lack the self-confidence to pursue their dreams. Or they're so identified with a victim persona that they don't know *how* to take responsibility for their lives and take initiative to create the life they dream of having.

The other factor here is that to a large degree, people respond to us by the level of self-confidence we exude. If the persona we present out in the world is one of insecurity or self-deprecation, people are not going to be very compelled to offer us job promotions, invest in our business, or engage with us in a personal or professional relationship.

Wright

Why is it so difficult for people to change and move beyond their core beliefs and habitual behaviors?

Mackler

The first thing is that many people are not even *aware* of the parts of them that carry their limiting beliefs and feelings about themselves and the world. When faced with feelings that threaten our well-being and ability to function, the human system will ingeniously find ways to diffuse or cover them up in order to survive. For example, if a child develops feelings of unworthiness (in response to his or her experiences and environment), these feelings, if severe enough, are so painful that they may cause him or her to develop a persona of arrogance to compensate for the part that feels worthless. These people may see themselves as better than other people and be perceived by others as ultra-confident or arrogant. This produces even more frustration for them because they think, "I'm smarter and more talented than John. I don't understand why *he's* the CEO and I'm not!" Core beliefs and habitual behaviors are rooted in the deeper, unconscious parts of us.

We cannot effectively change them unless we become fully aware of what they are, where they originate, and the results they produce.

One thing I'd like people to understand is that they shouldn't judge themselves for their limiting beliefs and behaviors because they served a real purpose in their lives. As children, our core beliefs and habitual behaviors enable us to adapt to and function within our family system, both of which are critical to our early survival. However, once we're grown and leave the family system to create our adult lives our needs, aspirations, and circumstances change. Hence, we need to "update" the core beliefs and habitual behaviors developed as children to align them with the new circumstances, experiences, and results to which we aspire as adults.

Wright

How do people go about updating their core beliefs and habitual behaviors to align them with goals they want to achieve?

Mackler

As I said earlier, the first step is getting clear about what they are. In all of my coaching programs, this is where we begin. First, I use a variety of assessment strategies to identify the client's habitual behaviors, including those which are predominant and those which the client activates less often. For example, a client who predominantly engages in approval-seeking behaviors will typically use self-asserting behaviors less often. Conversely, if a client predominantly engages in controlling or intimidating behaviors, he or she will engage in approval-seeking behaviors less often. These behaviors are important to identify because they either foster or hinder people's success. For example, if someone is a habitual approval-seeker, he or she will tend to focus on meeting other people's needs and expectations, versus attending to those of his or her own. As a result, approval-seekers often have difficulty identifying their own needs and goals because their focus has been on others and not on themselves. Or they may be clear about their goals but unable to pursue them out of fear of others' disapproval or judgment of them.

Once we've identified the clients' habitual behaviors we do an analysis of their family of origin. This entails identifying the attributes of the clients' family systems, their primary role in their family, the positive and negative attributes of the parents or primary caretakers, and how they felt growing up. We then use this information, along with habitual behaviors, to uncover core beliefs internalized about the world and themselves in response to these childhood influences.

Next I use a therapeutic technique called Voice Dialogue, during which I engage and talk to the different parts of the client that hold the limiting beliefs and drive his or her habitual behaviors. I use Voice Dialogue as it is the most effective form of talk therapy I've found that can help the client move beyond his or her automatic defense mechanisms and access the deeper levels of the unconscious (which is where the core beliefs and habitual behaviors are rooted). This allows clients to have not only an *intellectual understanding* of the parts of themselves that sabotage their success, but to gain *experientially-based knowledge* of how these parts operate, when they came into being, why they were needed, and the results they produce in their current lives. This experience also allows clients to move from self-judgment into greater understanding of and compassion toward themselves.

The next step is to articulate a clear vision statement that summarizes what the client wants to achieve in his or her life. The vision statement is a tool designed to focus the client's conscious and unconscious mind, energy, and resources to achieve a specific goal or desired future state. A teacher of mine once said, "Where you focus is where you go." We use the vision statement to maintain focus and as a constant reference point against everything the client does: "Is this taking me closer to or farther away from what I want in my life?"

Once the vision is articulated we identify the new behaviors and supporting beliefs needed to achieve it. We also identify things the client can put in his or her physical environment as reminders to activate the new beliefs and behaviors when the old ones resurface. These might be buying and wearing a specific piece of jewelry or putting inspirational pictures or objects in the home and work environment.

I've personally used different things to help me stay focused on new beliefs and behaviors. For example, one of my own limiting beliefs was that I needed a man to keep me safe and secure in life. This core belief, which had been ingrained in me since I was very little, created a lot of fear when I decided to leave my marriage. In support of the new belief that I wanted to internalize, which was, "I am a powerful and creative woman, fully capable of caring for myself," I bought and hung a picture of a woman who was half woman and half eagle, perched high on a mountain and ready to take off in flight. The picture represented the new belief I needed to internalize in order to pursue a new life on my own, and it deepened my motivation to more fully develop and express the powerful and creative part of me out in the world.

Wright

In addition to developing a vision and activating the beliefs and behaviors needed to bring the vision to reality, what else can people do to achieve greater success?

Mackler

Well, there are a couple of other components we haven't yet discussed that are critical to achieving success. The first is to develop a concrete action plan for achieving your life vision. It's taking the principles of sound business planning and translating them into strategic life planning. These include identifying specific, measurable, action-oriented, realistic, and time-bound goals and action steps that need to be taken in pursuit of the vision. Examples might be: "Complete my graduate degree by May 31, 2007." "Develop and start adhering to a daily exercise plan by February 1, 2007." "Choose two social activities where I can meet new people on a weekly basis by February 15, 2007." Having a vision is powerful, but without specific goals and a concrete plan for achieving it, you won't be able to bring it to fruition.

And last but not least, another factor that influences our level of success is the degree to which we develop an inner and outer support system. Developing an inner support system is done by taking good care of ourselves, thereby creating the inner resources needed to activate our vision and action plan. This is done by eating nutritious, energy-giving food, getting plenty of sleep, exercising, meditating, having a healthy work/life balance, and other activities that replenish our physical, mental, emotional, and spiritual health.

An outer support system is created by surrounding ourselves with people who are loving, compassionate, and kind, who support and encourage us in the pursuit of our life goals. However, since we tend to pull people into our lives who treat us as we treat ourselves, an important first step in creating a strong outer support system is to first develop a loving and supportive relationship with ourselves.

Wright

We have been talking with Lauren Mackler. Lauren has helped thousands of people to better understand the roots of the limiting beliefs and habitual behaviors that hinder activation of their potential, and how to develop new beliefs and behaviors needed to produce the results they seek in their personal and professional lives.

I've gained a lot of new insights from this interview, Lauren, and want to thank you so much for spending so much time with me and answering these questions for *Speaking of Success*.

Mackler

It's always a joy to be able to share this information with others, so I thank you very much for having me.

About the Author

One of America's leading coaches, Lauren Mackler has inspired people to reach the next level of success since 1982. She is frequently interviewed by *The Wall Street Journal*, *Boston Globe*, and *Boston Business Journal*, and other publications, television, and radio. Her company, Lauren Mackler & Associates, was recognized as one of the top five coaching firms in the United States and the best in Boston by *Vitals Magazine*. Lauren founded LMA in 2001, providing coaching programs, workshops, and consulting services that help clients to unleash their greatest potential in their personal lives, careers, relationships, and organizations.

Lauren Mackler & Associates LLC
Phone: 617.244.6420
E-mail: info@laurenmackler.com
www.laurenmackler.com

Chapter 4

CYNTHIA STOTLAR

David Wright (Wright)

Today we are talking with Cynthia Stotlar. For over fifteen years Cynthia has helped clients improve their bottom line and customer satisfaction with a mix of high value consulting and training services. Over 150 companies have benefited from her approach and over 15,000 participants have attended her dynamic presentations.

Prior to founding Creative Business Solutions, Cynthia worked for large organizations in human resources, quality improvement, operations, and training. With a master's in Adult Education and certifications from both SHRM and ASTD, Cynthia brings the right mix of real world experience and professional training to bear on client needs. Cynthia has co-authored two previous books and countless articles.

Cynthia, welcome to *Speaking of Success.*

Cynthia, how do you define success?

Cynthia Stotlar (Stotlar)

Success is being lucky enough to get paid for what you love doing! Ultimately, success is being able to leave the world better than you found it. I do that through working with business leaders to help their companies perform better and provide more motivating work environments.

I agree with Henry David Thoreau who said, "We were born to succeed, not to fail." I think each of us do have the potential to be successful, yet everyone who is successful has gotten there by taking risks and failing first. One of life's many ironies is that to become successful, you must fail.

Wright

What is the biggest contribution to your professional success?

Wright

Being willing to change, having an insatiable desire to learn new things, and a willingness to work hard are huge contributors.

I think all of us switch on our personal "autopilot" from time to time and coast. And some people retire on the job while still drawing a paycheck. We need to reevaluate how we are doing things and whether we are getting the desired results. An insatiable desire to learn new things certainly helps. The world is changing at an amazing rate. We have to be willing to pick up new techniques, new equipment, and use those to our advantage. You can't stay on autopilot.

Being willing to work hard and long hours is a huge contributor. One of the people I met when I was starting my business laughed and said, "As an entrepreneur, you get flexible hours—you get to choose which twelve hours of the day you want to work, the first twelve or the last twelve! Success rarely comes without effort. Henry Ford said the reason many opportunities are missed is because they come dressed looking like work. But so many things came together to make it all work. Had we not moved to Topeka, it is unlikely I would ever have started my own business. Topeka's business community is welcoming and supportive of entrepreneurs. Without my husband joining the business six years ago, I doubt we would have grown the business to where it is today.

Wright

You've talked about people who influenced your life, like your parents, grandmothers, Ken Blanchard, Stephen Covey, and Tom Peters. How can people help other people succeed?

Stotlar

Interestingly, I think many help others succeed unknowingly by simply taking a genuine interest in them. I've tremendously admired many of the people I've worked for or with and used them as role models. I doubt many ever realized that I was looking to them for wisdom or insight.

Role modeling, taking time to share ideas, being a sounding board, and offering advice are all great ways to help others succeed. Writing books such as this that provide insight into how you succeeded helps. The first management book I ever read was *One Minute Manager* by Blanchard. The next year I was lucky enough to see Dr. Blanchard discuss his ideas at a seminar. I was mesmerized as I realized that we'd all be so much more effective as managers if the concepts were presented in a down-to-earth, understandable way. Without knowing it, he inspired me first to become a better manager and second to share practical ideas with others. It was an epiphany for me that management should flex their style to fit the situation and person's needs. So without knowing it, he inspired me to become a better manager. Our consulting is also built around practical ideas and solutions rather than "pie in the sky," and they work!

But sometimes it's the push or challenge you didn't know you were ready for or the denial of an opportunity you thought you were ready for that spurs you on to personal improvement. These events push you to "ponder" your life and its true meaning.

My first manager, Dr. Mason, pushed me to become my personal best. He challenged me to take call for the evening and night shifts. I did not want to let him down. I studied everything I could find and became a board-certified specialist in blood banking to make sure late night questions were answered to the very best of my ability. His push drove me to become more successful in my job and significantly more confident in my skills.

Another turn in the road was a denied opportunity. I was told I didn't have good enough communication or conflict resolution skills when I first asked to be considered for a supervisor position. That denial spurred me to better develop both skill sets. In a year I was promoted to management. That became a foundation for the work I do now.

So you can help people succeed in a number of ways. You probably have already done so and just don't know it. I've been told by many people that they have modeled my behavior when they find themselves in similar situations. I wasn't trying to be role model. I was simply doing the best I could with what I had at the time.

Wright

Tell me, what is a performance improvement consultant?

Stotlar

Performance consulting looks at the current or real performance versus the desired performance and identifies ways to move a person, a department, a team, or even an entire company closer to their desired or ideal performance. It goes far beyond individual coaching as we look at systems, processes, and people.

Part of being successful is gaining the knowledge you need to be successful at your chosen career. For example, I have completed the American Society of Training and Development's (ASTD) Human Performance Improvement certificate program. I also have a master's in adult education and am a senior professional in human resources.

We adapted the ASTD Human Performance Improvement Model (HPI) to include continuous communication and continuous change management throughout the five phases. The HPI model includes:

1. Analyzing performance
2. Determining underlying causes of non-performance
3. Selecting interventions that will move the person, team or organization toward the goals
4. Implementating improvement strategies
5. Evaluating the process to determine its effectiveness

We look for ways to improve the situation to meet the desired goals. We also look for ways to use each person's talents to the max. If you can match employee strengths and talents with the right job description, you will move the organization further and faster than trying to mold employees to fit the job.

We use assessments from Profiles International to identify underlying people issues and develop coaching plans. Profiles International has several marvelous tools for consultants. The Personal Profile Indicator™ and Team Analysis™ are superb tools for use either as a coach or when working with a team. Their Checkpoint 360 Degree Feedback Assessment™ is excellent when identifying management behaviors.

We combine these tools with our own employee engagement survey to measure the pulse of employees. We also audit management and HR functions and processes to determine how overall goals and strategy are set plus how the performance appraisal process, compensation, and rewards influence outcomes.

These assessments and tools provide objective rather than subjective data. They provide baselines so that you can look to see whether you really have made a difference or not.

Wright

How is a performance improvement consultant different from being a coach?

Stotlar

There is definitely some overlap. When we work with one person as a performance consultant, coaching occurs. When we are working with a team or department, we often spend more time with the team leader or department head to move improvements. When we work with an organization, we partner with the CEO or Executive Director. However, performance improvement kicks coaching up a notch in the sense that you look at a bigger picture than just any one person. We deal with the entire system including processes, performance management tools, incentives, and rewards.

For example, one organization wanted teams to identify improvement opportunities. They put some systems in place that they thought would support teamwork, but they had forgotten to change their performance appraisal system to reward and recognize teamwork. The system actually "dinged" employees for being away from their desks, so nobody was coming to the team meetings. If we had been coaching, we probably would have been talking to that one manager about how to get more people to come to his team meetings. But that wouldn't have helped because the issue was a system issue. When we modified their performance appraisal system to recognize and reward teamwork the problem was solved.

Wright

When people follow their passion and excel at it, would you say that the passion brings the success or the success brings the passion?

Stotlar

Personally, I think its one of those "never to be answered" questions like "which came first—the chicken or the egg?" You need passion to succeed. Whether it is your passion for hamburger that leads to a new McDonald's or your passion for that perfect cup of coffee that starts a new Starbucks, you need the passion to stay in the game when times are tough and you run into obstacles.

Conversely, if you do a task successfully and get positive recognition for it, passion can come from having been successful. I didn't have a passion for training initially; in fact, I consciously choose not to become teacher in college. But when forced to train others I was complimented for doing a good job and having potential. I developed that potential and the passion followed that still sustains me over thirty years later.

My passion is for helping make things better in business. I get jazzed when management succeeds while maintaining the dignity of employees. I get jazzed when employees suddenly enjoy their jobs more fully and out-perform their previous best.

Wright

What makes your perspective unique?

Stotlar

Our philosophy is to help people build on strengths and manage "improvement opportunities." I was lucky enough to work for Derrick Suehs. He was the organization's Director of Organizational Development and worked from the philosophy that we should focus on the employees who were already good. We helped them get better and trained those who actually wanted to learn. This experience taught me that you will get further faster with those who want to improve. It's like the old joke, "How many psychiatrists does it take to change a lightbulb? Only one, but the lightbulb has to want to change."

We can help people improve their personal performance, their department's performance, and the company's performance, but they have to be willing to make changes and look at the situation from a different perspective.

Marcus Buckingham's work in *First Break All the Rules* confirmed that focusing on your high-potential employees gets companies to high performance with less energy than trying to bring up the bottom performers. Yet sadly in today's workplace, we usually spend 80 percent of our time coaching and counseling the bottom 20 percent. We want you to put that same time and energy into your top 20 percent and see what happens. As Eric Hoffer said, "We are told that talent creates its own opportunities. But it sometimes seems that intense desire creates not only its own opportunities, but its own talents." Your top 20 percent have that intense desire.

Likewise when we are coaching employees, we identify their strengths and their passions and look for ways to build on those.

Wright

What brings you the most personal satisfaction, professional satisfaction?

Stotlar

Personally, I enjoy solving problems creatively and exploring new ideas. We have been fortunate enough to have traveled abroad. Your perspective changes after having spent time in Africa, Costa Rica, Italy, or Ireland. I have learned much from many different cultures and that has helped me appreciate life's diversity even more. It also gives unique insights. Travel has helped me become a far better communicator, facilitator, and consultant.

Painting is a personal passion. While painting, I allow my subconscious to process and it frequently comes up with more creative approaches than when I'm in the office.

Professionally, it is when I am working with someone one-on-one or in a classroom setting and the lightbulb goes on. That is tremendously satisfying. It's like winning the lottery when a client calls and lets us know that his or her team is working more effectively together or that the organization has just posted a huge increase in productivity or profitability.

Wright

How does your work impact your clients?

Stotlar

For one organization, we worked with their customer service team to help them become more sales oriented. They wanted the traditional up-sell concepts, but their staff members weren't salespeople, they were drivers and considered themselves service staff. So we worked with them to make up-selling and cross-selling a "service activity." After three months they had outperformed every other business unit in the United States in sales! And that included business units in cities like Los Angeles that are 100 times larger!

Another company—a large non-profit—reduced their employee turnover by 52 percent, which put over $250K back on the bottom line. That has the ripple effect of allowing them to better serve their clients and fulfill their mission.

Since our work affects how businesses treat their employees, we like to think that we are having huge positive ripples in the community.

Wright

What tips would you give to others seeking personal success?

Stotlar

Do what you love, love what you do, and help others become their personal best. Take risks. When you fail, learn from your mistakes, and keep trying.

In business as in life, success goes to those prepared to achieve. We do a "lessons learned" de-briefing after each project to determine what worked well and what we can do better next time. We start each staff meeting with "celebrations and congratulations" because we want to remember to thank each other and celebrate the many successes we have throughout the process. At every staff meeting we look for ways to improve our service to our clients and to ourselves as internal customers. There is always room for improvement.

You must be willing to change your business model and/or services to better meet client needs. We started out just providing customized training. Now, fourteen years later, we consult more, train less, and offer full outsourced HR. We work to analyze business trends and be ready for the next new thing before our clients want it. Benjamin Disraeli once said, "The secret of success in life is for a man to be ready for his opportunity when it comes."

Wright

When you consider opportunities, what do you think is going to happen with you and your company in the next few years? Have you got any new things that you'll introduce; do you keep doing the same things and get better? What does the future look like for you?

Stotlar

In the past two years, we have moved to providing full outsourced HR. We can do everything an in-house HR department would do for a company. We can either do project work such as revamp your performance appraisal system, deal with your employer relations issues, survey employee engagement, or we can actually do "soup to nuts" HR. We can hire your employees, do payroll, and more. We anticipate that part of our business will be growing.

We are looking to put anything and everything that we can online for easy access. People want 24/7 access—having office hours only between eight to five o'clock isn't going to work long-term. So we are actively looking for ways to make those kinds of things happen.

Successful people, and businesses, have to flex to changing needs. We hope to be flexing for a long time to come.

Wright

I love to talk to people who have plans. It sounds like you're staying in business not going out of business.

Stotlar

Yes, we are staying in business. We hope to continue to grow the business and hand it down to the next generation of consultants we are now grooming.

Wright

What a great conversation. I've learned a lot today about the different ways of coaching and training and I appreciate your spending all this time answering these questions for me.

Stotlar

You are most welcome.

Wright

Today, we have been talking with Cynthia Stotlar. For fifteen years she has been helping clients improve their bottom line and helping them increase customer satisfaction with her training and consulting services. Over 150 companies have benefited from her approach and over 15,000 participants have attended her dynamic presentations. After our conversation here I see why. She knows what she's talking about.

Thank you so much, Cynthia, for being with us today on *Speaking of Success.*

Stotlar
You're welcome.

About the Author

For over fifteen years Cynthia has helped clients improve their bottom line and customer satisfaction with a mix of high value consulting and training services. Over 15,000 participants have attended her dynamic presentations. She is a certified trainer for both DDI and Achieve Global, bringing a ton of fun along with very practical ideas into the classroom.

Prior to founding Creative Business Solutions, Cynthia worked for large organizations in human resources, quality improvement, operations, and training. With a Master's in Adult Education, Cynthia is also certified as a Senior Human Resource professional by Human Resources Certification Institute and as a Human Performance Improvement Consultant by the American Society of Training and Development.

Cynthia brings the right mix of real world experience and professional training to bear on client needs. Cynthia has co-authored two previous books, *Career Compass for Women* and *Power Tools for Success*, and countless articles.

Cynthia and her company can assist your company improve your HR processes, hiring practices, customer service, sales, executive and leadership development, succession planning, overall productivity and profitability, and bottom line!

Cynthia B. Stotlar, M.Ed, SPHR
Creative Business Solutions
5315 SW 7th Street
Topeka Kansas 66606
Phone: 785.233.7860
www.CBSKS.com

Chapter 5

CHRIS WAUGH

David Wright (Wright)

Today we are talking with Chris Waugh. She owns reNvision Inc. and gives professionals an aerial perspective on change, success, leadership, and motivation. She shows her clients how to succeed "on the fly."

Chris's management background spans three decades, yet it's her experience as an advanced hang glider pilot that really stretches her perspective. Her keynote speeches, training, coaching, and consulting deliver insights from solid ground, the edge, and sometimes over the edge.

She's the author of *Flying by the Seat of Your Pants*, a self-help success book, *Misty Memories of Guard Island,* an historical memoir on change, and *Updrafts: Insights that Lend Wings to Your Success.* She is writing a leadership book titled, *Flying in the Face of Conventional Wisdom*. She also hosts *Success: The Sky's the Limit*, a weekly radio talk show.

Chris, welcome to *Speaking of Success.*

Waugh

Thank you, David it's great to have the opportunity to discuss my favorite topic—success.

Wright

Your company name is reNvision. Would you tell our readers what you mean by that?

Waugh

The name reNvision is a verb, like re-envision. It means to take another look—to shift your focus and see things from a different perspective. When you reNvision, you reanalyze and you reinvigorate and reinvent yourself as well as your relationships, your organizations, and even your community.

Life is full of lessons to learn and insights that help you grow. But you have to pay attention, so to reNvision takes mindfulness. Sometimes you think you know but you don't—your mind can play tricks on you. That's why optical illusions can fool you so easily. Perhaps you can remember a time when you've been driving a car and stopped at a traffic light; the car next to you started to roll forward. You saw it out of your peripheral vision, but you thought you were moving, so you stepped on the break. Your body and your mind play these kinds of tricks.

Sometimes you can misinterpret other people's body language. You might think their closed posture means they are mad but maybe they are just cold. So you really have to remember to reNvision. Reexamine. Don't overlook the obvious. The answer could be right under your nose. Instead of seeing the problem, you can be discovering hidden opportunities within those problems if you reNvision.

Wright

You talk a lot about changing your perspective. Why is that so important for our success?

Waugh

We become creatures of habit. Habits help us because they simplify our lives and our focus. If it wasn't for our ability to focus, we'd become overwhelmed with stimuli. A newborn baby stares everywhere and nowhere at the same time with his mouth agape. That's an example of a lack of focus. There is *so* much to take in. If you didn't learn to focus, you'd probably go crazy, so you have to learn to focus.

However, remember that every time you focus on one thing, you are screening out many other factors and possibilities.

I remember taking a walk with my nephew, Jared. He had just moved to rural Oregon from an urban environment and I was going to teach him how to find mushrooms. I told him what they looked like and to look on the ground for them. Now, he was only four-years-old at the time and he wasn't focused at all. He kept playing with the bugs and climbing the trees and splashing in the puddles. He was looking everywhere except on the ground where I told him the mushrooms were. I was getting frustrated. I started to scold him when I saw him gazing up a tree with this question in his eyes and he stopped me and pointed up the trunk. There were a hundred mushrooms growing up there. I later learned they were oyster mushrooms which are choice edibles and expensive mushrooms if you buy them in the grocery store. I had never found those mushrooms before because I had always looked only on the ground. I had never looked up.

We tend to walk with our heads down. We look at the ground and not at the world around us. Occasionally it's good to look up to "reN-vision" and change your perspective for several reasons: You might re-verify your assumptions—make sure the things that you think are true indeed are true. You might want to reconfirm your heading to see that you are going in the direction you want to go. When you reN-vision and re-verify, you re-energize yourself and you add momentum to your journey.

Wright

You're author of *Flying by the Seat of Your Pants,* a self-help success book with a very novel approach. In it you say that knowing how to "wing it" effectively is the key to success. Will you tell us about that?

Waugh

As I was writing this book, I remember telling people that I was writing a book with the title, *Flying by the Seat of Your Pants.* Their reactions were frequently the same. They would shyly look down with embarrassment and shuffle their feet and admit to me, "I feel like I'm flying by the seat of my pants all the time," as if it was a bad thing to do. Today, people associate "winging it" with a haphazard approach to life. It seems flippant or unorganized to make it all up as you go along—not to have plans and strategies. How can one possibly succeed that way?

In the early days of aviation, flying by the seat of your pants was the way it was done. Pilots would nimbly respond to the conditions that they perceived and guide the glider or airplane accordingly. These days, when you board a jet airplane, the pilot tells you where you're going, what altitude you'll be flying, and when you'll land. In life though, your "flight" is similar to earlier aviation, or like mine when I'm flying my hang glider. You don't always know where you are going to land.

The term "flying by the seat of your pants" has a bad reputation and I think it's unfair. I'm on a mission to change the way people think about it. I have always been frustrated by traditional goal-setting strategies. We are taught to plan our work and work our plan—that our goals should be precise, measurable, written, and dated, and we should have a crystal-clear vision of our destination and devise a map to get there. And then I'm sure you've heard this one: "Always keep your eyes on the goal."

I think those concepts are fine if you're going to Disneyland. Know where you're going, measure the distance, calculate your miles per gallon, and map out your route. But seeing the future isn't as concrete as a trip to Disneyland, or is it as static.

Your future is dynamic, it's fluid, and it's turbulent like the wind. Here are five reasons to learn "flying by the seat of your pants:"

1. Your world isn't concrete—it's space and energy. It's not like going from point A to point B. It's more like searching for the end of the rainbow. There is no "there." Sometimes you don't want what you thought you wanted by the time you reach your goal. Things change and so do you.
2. You might not have a specific goal. Many of us don't exactly know what we want to do when we grow up. I'm not sure I do and I'm fifty-five! I'm still evolving, and that's okay.
3. You are time pressured and stressed out because the time it takes to set these specific strategies is often more than the time you have to spare. You think you should be mapping out your plans. You don't have time so you stress out about it and you end up frustrated and exhausted.
4. You are overlooking opportunities when you try to stay focused on your goals. You fly right past potential.

   I remember flying my hang glider across a valley one time to reach a thermal that I had spotted. I thought it would be the mother of all thermals, and to get to it I passed through several other updrafts. By the time I reached my perfect one, it had dissipated. When you get too goal focused, you're overlooking opportunities; you're flying right through them. And they don't wait for your return.

5. Your plans don't always work. It's impossible to anticipate everything that might happen. How many of your New Year's resolutions are ever achieved? Usually very few.

I conducted a survey of successful business professionals and asked them this question, "When you were in kindergarten or even when you were in high school, what did you plan to be when you grew up?" And then I asked, "Were you right? Is that what you are doing now?" How about you, David? What were you going to be? Were you going to be an author and a publisher?

Wright

Not even close.

Waugh

See? In my surveys, *98 percent of us* are not doing what we thought we'd be doing. We've all been flying by the seat of our pants. You resist that notion because you think it's wrong. You want to think that traditional goal-setting will give you some control over your destiny and lead you to success. You don't think of yourself as a pilot in your life and you don't learn how to wing it. If you reNvision the concept of flying by the seat of your pants, you can succeed much more easily.

Wright

So we don't have to take up hang gliding to learn what pilots know about succeeding on the fly?

Waugh

No. Thankfully you don't have to strap yourself into a hang glider like I do and run off a cliff. You'll find, though, that the concept translates very well into everyday life.

You've been in the pilot's seat all along, you just need a pilot's manual. So instead of the conventional goal-setting strategies, let's discuss these replacement adages: be aware and prepared, but only make a *general* flight plan; your goals don't have to be specific—they'll probably change anyway; your destinations matter less than the quality of your flight; and finally, *always* keep your eyes open for opportunities. You can take the concepts that enable hang glider pilots to soar and practice them in life. There are three overlapping elements that hang glider pilots put into practice to wing it effectively.

Wright

So what are those three elements?

Waugh

Be aware, prepare, and dare. They even rhyme so they are easier to remember.

First you have to be aware. This step requires a keen insight and level of understanding of yourself. Most people don't have their awareness refined to a high enough level. You will learn to use your senses better. This is where you start and you spend a *great* deal of focus. In fact, this is where you spend *most* of your energy—being aware.

The next step is to prepare. You're going to be navigating through some unfamiliar territory. It's called the future. It's turbulent and it has threats and opportunities. You must be prepared physically and mentally for the voyage and understand the dynamics and the variables. It involves learning and stretching.

But many would-be pilots stop there. They fail to take the third step—to dare. They don't make the commitment. They are like the bride who runs away from the wedding after choosing the dress, the flowers, and sending out the invitations. They may be like the person with the new ski gear I've seen sitting in the lodge all day and never venturing out on the slope. They are like the college student who still only needs two more credits to graduate. And finally, they are like an office assistant who hasn't asked for the well-deserved raise because the time isn't perfect. The dare is the hardest part but the dare is where the growth occurs. The dare is the launch on the journey.

These three elements sound simple—to be aware, prepare, and dare. Make a determined and a conscious effort to discipline yourself to put them to use.

Wright

Let's take those one at a time and find out more about what you mean by them. Can you first explain "be aware?"

Waugh

Understanding our world takes constant observation. You look at yourself, at the other pilots, and at the environment with an objective to see it non-judgmentally. The more you observe, the more you see; the more you see, the more you understand; and the more you understand, the better you can maneuver on the fly. So don't minimize this first element. In fact, I don't think it's possible to be too aware. Your awareness has four aspects: self-awareness, awareness of others, and the laws of weather and flight.

First know yourself. Now, *that* one can be the most difficult, but you need to understand what makes *you* tick. Respect yourself. Realize that *your* motivations are different and utilize *your* strengths and based on those things, you set a heading.

Next, recognize that other people are on different but no less important flight paths. They may have different motivations. You need to respect them too. If you are working together in a business, or on a team, the results are more effective if those flight paths are parallel. Everyone has to be aware of the group purpose. Everyone must be focused in the same direction.

Third, pay attention to the climate around you—which way the wind blows so to speak. Respect Mother Nature. You live and work in this environment—the economy, the corporate culture, and the future, all of which are like the weather. You'll be looking for opportunities.

And finally, you'll want to understand the dynamics of flight. You have to know how to take advantage of the potential. You'll want to be an expert at maneuvering.

Wright

It sounds as if you put the emphasis on being aware. Why is that?

Waugh

You're right. I think you should spend the bulk of your time honing your awareness. If you're like the rest of us, you probably have too close a view of yourself and that's why your life seems larger than life. Your problems are bigger, your failures are bigger, your needs are more urgent, and your fears are worse. As human beings we can be so dramatic. On the other hand, maybe you are the opposite. Maybe you know everyone *else* better than you know yourself. You haven't taken time to know yourself as a person. What interests *you?* What motivates you? What do you avoid at all costs? And why do you react to certain situations the way you do?

Orville Wright said, "Learning the secrets of flight from a bird was a good deal like learning the secrets of magic from a magician. After you know what to look for, you see things that you did not notice when you did not know exactly what to look for."

You have an autopilot just like many airplanes. On one hand it's a wonderful navigational aide. It allows you to do repetitive tasks without conscious thought, like tying your shoes or signing your name. Unfortunately, many people fly through their whole lives on autopilot. Be aware of this tendency. Use your mind on purpose. Decide when to let autopilot take control and when *you* need to be in charge.

Spend time figuring out what's important to you—what really matters. What do you like to do and what are you good at? You want to be aware of where you are now and where you would like to go. This is typically called vision and values. But I also want you to reconsider your self-image. Is it respectful or is it judgmental and full of criticism? Be rational with yourself. How perfect do you have feel about yourself to create a healthy self-image?

As a pilot, you have many key areas to be aware of: what excites you, where you want to go, how you see the world, what limitations you have, and which ones are self-imposed?

When I started flying hang gliders, women didn't fly. We were thought to be too weak. Well, I just had to change the *way* I approached flight and I learned that indeed girls can be very good pilots.

What is your tolerance of risk? Do you take responsibility for your results? As a pilot, you have to. The point here is not to judge yourself as much as it is to inventory yourself. Really understand yourself. If you know your own values, strengths, weaknesses, delights, and fears you can accommodate and use them more effectively. You need to have your priorities straight if you are going to fly hang gliders or thrive in this changing world.

Emphasize your strengths and delights. Some people spend too much time trying to improve their weaknesses and manage their fears. That is a waste of time. Focus on the positive. You get more out of your energy that way and besides, you have more fun doing it. You're rare and special just the way you are. You're unique and evolving. You have to be kind and objective and understand yourself. Self-awareness is *so* important. I spend so much time there, but let me touch on the other three aspects of awareness.

Other pilots are on different paths. They may or may not be aware of themselves and their motivations. Some of them form your support structure like a vehicle driver does for a hang glider pilot. You might have friends and mentors and other types of supporters. Other people, though, may not be there for you at all and you need to be aware of their motives.

Another thing hang glider pilots know is that there are also physical laws that cannot be argued. The weather is a good example. It will probably change tomorrow, so there is no point in bemoaning what should have been. The world around you is the same way. You have to know how to fly in the weather that exists today. You can't always wait for the ideal situation—it might never happen.

The dynamics of flight are simple, and that's the fourth thing. First, your attitude must be right. Just like the wing of an aircraft, if it's too positive—up too high—the wing stalls and there is a loss of control. I think people with overly optimistic attitudes lose control too and they can be blindsided and defeated easily when adversity strikes. If, however, their wing attitude is too negative, the wing will dive. The object here is to soar. You want to rise up and a neutral or slightly positive attitude is always optimum, in flying and in life.

People ask me how to produce lift in flight. Lift is just the balance of three other forces: gravity, momentum, and drag. And you have those forces in life too. Gravity keeps you grounded—it's your family, your values, and your beliefs. Your momentum is your self-awareness and your heading—it's where you want to go and the energy you put into going there.

And there is always drag. I don't usually have to explain that one. Drag keeps you from going forward and it offsets your momentum. The more momentum you have, the more drag you experience. If you have the attitude right and the proper mix of gravity, momentum, and drag, you actually produce lift and you can soar higher and succeed.

All of these essentials make up that first element: be aware.

Wright
And once we're aware we're better able to prepare?

Waugh

Right. Too many times I am dealing with boards of directors whose members want to quickly review their mission statement and jump right into preparation. I always have to hold them back. If you don't *really* understand *why* you're going where you're going, you might be preparing for the wrong thing.

You have to understand how and what to prepare. Pilots go to ground school where they study the basics. Then they go to the training hill where they start to grow. And they make many choices along the way. Our learning and growth happens on a continuum, between bored to death and scared to death. Neither extreme is healthy or fun. Let's examine the area in the middle. You have a comfort zone toward the bored end of that spectrum. You know your skill and you can perform it on autopilot. In fact, it's comfortable. You don't grow there, however, and you don't learn. When you push yourself up and out of that area, you move into what I call "the stretch zone" where you aren't as comfortable anymore, but you aren't scared to death either. You are stimulated.

If you stretch too far, you enter the panic zone and at that point, you lose your ability to concentrate and perform. Let me use the example of the hang gliding training hill. Usually it's a sand dune. At first you can barely hold up that heavy glider and keep it stable. Soon, that becomes easy so you try to walk and then you try to run with it on the level beach. You keep stretching until you master that. Now you climb up the sand dune just a little and you try to run down hoping to just get a few inches off the ground. Usually, the first few times you don't hold your glider right and you fall down. Hang glider pilots call that process "eating sand."

Once you learn to keep the attitude correct though, you can actually get to the point of skimming the ground and you get a few feet of air as you glide down the beach. And then with new found confidence, you venture farther up the sand dune. Each time you stretch farther you make new mistakes and you eventually conquer them. That's when that level becomes comfortable and it's time to stretch again. And that's how I think you learn anything.

The trouble is that after a while you want to stay in your comfort zone. You start avoiding risks. You forget the thrill of the stretch. You miss out on the exhilaration of learning and you don't grow anymore. So keep stretching—it's not just for exercise.

Another important element in preparing is what pilots call "staying current." Studies show that if you learn a skill, you forget most of it right away. If you relearn it, it takes almost a week to forget most of it. And if you relearn it again, the skill stays fresh with you for maybe a month. Each time you top off your knowledge, you extend its usefulness. You always have to keep it current.

In hang gliding, most tragic accidents happen during take off and landing, because, as they say, "you don't get hurt until you hit the ground"—you're close to the ground during take off and landing. Flying the glider is easy, you just hang there and it flies. But these two skills are the basic in every flight because you have to launch and you have to land. If you don't practice those skills you get sloppy, you get rusty, and that can spell disaster; so good pilots practice. They practice doing "touch and goes"—they practice take-off and landing basics to keep themselves current.

You have basic skills you use every day at home and at work; skills like communication and conflict resolution, teamwork, leadership, sales, customer service, and the list goes on. You need to continually hone those skills or they get stagnant. To wing it effectively, you won't have time to stop and think about those basic techniques. You have to perform them flawlessly and automatically, and on the fly. So don't let the basics get rusty.

Like most pilots you make choices along the way: your alliances, your equipment, and your timing, just to name a few. As pilot of *your* success, make those choices carefully. It's all about pilot responsibility. You can't blame others, you can't blame the glider, and you can't blame the weather.

A hang glider pilot usually has a flexible flight plan, but not a strict one like a commercial airliner pilot might file, because in a hang glider, if opportunity presents itself, you'll want to be nimble enough to change course and take advantage of it. The same goes for your success.

When I coach high school students on career planning, I tell them not to get too specific in their career choice. Instead, I want them to choose a heading that suits their passion and then stay open to opportunities. New careers are popping up all the time. Most of us aren't doing what we thought we would be doing anyway. If you keep learning, stretching, and staying current on the basics and you make good choices, you'll be more likely to wing it successfully.

Wright

So flying by the seat of your pants doesn't necessarily mean being unprepared?

Waugh

Exactly. *That* is the misunderstanding about flying by the seat of your pants. People assume it means you shoot from the hip—you're unprepared. They think winging it means that you just show up and fake it. Let me assure you, when I fly my hang glider, I am ultra prepared. And I'm not just prepared for where I think I'm going—I am prepared for *anything*. I am ready to land where I anticipate. I am also ready to land short of my destination and maybe hike my glider out to where I can meet my driver. And, I am ready with extra food and water in case I get lucky and catch a powerful thermal that takes me so high that I can fly for miles cross-country.

If you are prepared for *anything*, you can mitigate the difficulties and take advantage of the opportunities you encounter. One day I had planned to launch off a mountain range and fly five miles out to a valley and land by the highway where the retrieval vehicle could easily find me. However, as I headed out I encountered turbulence. Some of it was very strong. I identified one big thermal in that bumpy air and started to circle tightly inside it. Soon I had gained over eight thousand feet of altitude. The landing area I had *planned* to land in was *two miles* below me at that point and what stretched out before me were miles of valley. The highway to the next state ran right in the middle of it. Why should I go down to the landing area when I could fly someplace new and exciting? I had a sandwich and some water in my pack and a two-way radio to communicate my change in plans so I ventured cross-country. Because I was prepared, I flew thirty-three miles that day. The old adage is true. Preparation and opportunity equals good luck.

Wright

So now I can guess what the dare is. You have to jump off the proverbial cliff, right?

Waugh

Yes. Daring is often equated with courage and that's true. It takes courage to dare. You have to face your fears; but daring is also the big payoff. It brings the reward—finally you get to fly! Daring is also associated with risk, yet the risk is alleviated if you are aware and prepared. That's why those two previous elements are *so* crucial in flying by the seat of your pants.

I remember once helping a fellow pilot launch. I held the nose of his glider while he got into his harness. I looked at his face and I saw incredible fear in his eyes. Either he wasn't really *aware* of his reason for flying or he was totally unprepared. Either way it was dangerous. He took up another sport after about a week and I was glad he did. He should not have been hang gliding. He would have been a statistic if he had continued.

Let me tell you about pilots, though, who are called "launch potatoes." They are similar to what you might think of as a couch potato only without the remote control. They are aware and prepared—they really are. They have the accoutrements of the sport and they are ready to launch. They stand at the launch ramp on the mountain and they wait. What are they waiting for? Often they want the perfect wind. Unfortunately, there is no such thing. It's like trying to wait for the perfect time to get married or the perfect time to have a child or start a business or ask for a raise. Don't wait for the perfect time. Simply wait for a good time. Then launch.

The flight part is the fun. Don't be so caught up in the mechanics of it that you forget to appreciate the view. Life is spectacular—enjoy the ride. Each journey is unique and special.

Each flight, though, eventually comes to an end. The landing zone is the end of the day. It's time to pack up and put away your toys. As you do, you want to reflect on the day's flight. Evaluate the venture, but don't beat yourself up over your mistakes. Simply learn from them. Plan a new way to approach them next time.

Finally, don't take yourself too seriously. Once I entered a competition with forty other hang glider pilots. I came in fourth and I was the only female. I was *pretty* proud of myself. In the landing area, as I was packing up my glider, another pilot behind me was folding up his glider. He glared at me and said, "I wish I had a woman to put *my* glider away." I was stunned. Didn't he know who I was? Didn't he know *I* was the only female in the competition and I had finished fourth and wasn't packing up a glider for somebody else? It was *my* glider! I thought of several snippy comebacks that would have really put this guy in his place. Then, thankfully, I stopped myself and I smiled. "Me too," I said. Everyone is winging it through life, even that pilot.

Wright

Knowing how to fly by the seat of your pants does sound like a better path to success in our turbulent world. But it doesn't sound like it's a straight line. How do you see our progress and approach toward success?

Waugh

You're right. To be aware, prepare, and dare does not form a linear path, David. You are never finished with any of the elements. Once you've dared, it's time to be aware again and then prepare for another flight. These three elements don't form a circle either because there is always something new for you to be aware of, prepare for, and dare to do. Nor do they form a nice even spiral upward toward success, however, that is a little closer to how they work.

When I core a thermal, I turn tight circles inside a column of rising air and it takes me up like a bumpy elevator. Seen from a distance, it looks like a smooth transition, but in reality it isn't. It's very turbulent. I might be going up steeply one second and then be pitched down the next. I have to fight to stay inside that thermal. It almost seems like it wants to spit me out.

Gaining altitude isn't easy or smooth; neither is life, neither is growth, and neither is success. Sometimes you have to step backward to go forward. Sometimes you face obstacles and have to try to penetrate or circumnavigate around them. Like the wind, your environment is never still; it's full of turbulence. But the lift is in the turbulence, just like the opportunities in life lie in its uncertainty. That's why by learning to fly by the seat of your pants you're more able to identify your opportunities and you are in a better position to take advantage of them. You'll have the confidence of a pilot—you *are* the pilot. You can soar. The hang gliding is optional.

Wright

Today we have been talking with Chris Waugh who owns reNvision Inc., and gives professionals an aerial perspective on change, success, leadership, and motivation. As we have found today, she knows a lot about flying. She's author of *Flying by the Seat of Your Pants*. I've paid attention to what she has to say here and I hope our readers do the same thing. I think she knows what she's talking about.

Thank you so much, Chris, for being with us today on *Speaking of Success*.

Waugh

You're welcome, David. I'm happy to have the opportunity to participate in this book project that is sure to lend wings to the success of our readers.

About the Author

CHRIS WAUGH is President of reNvision, Inc., and provides resources that lend wings to others' success. Her clients are professionals who want to learn to wing it successfully. They get practical insights from her keynotes, consulting, and training sessions. Chris has published three books, dozens of articles, and she hosts a weekly radio show, *Success: The Sky's the Limit.* She is grounded by decades of down-to-earth management experience, but she has the perspective of an advanced hang glider pilot that is edgy, and sometimes over the edge. She is a professional member of the National Speakers Association and a charter member of the United States Hang Gliding Association.

Visit www.reNvision.com to purchase additional copies of this book, or for more information and resources.

Chris Waugh, President
reNvision, Inc.
130 NW 19th Street A3
Newport, OR 97365
Phone: 541.270.0399
E-mail: Chriswaugh@reNvision.com
www.reNvision.com

Chapter 6

VAL BALDWIN, CPC

THE INTERVIEW

David Wright (Wright)

Today we're talking with Val Baldwin, professional speaker, trainer, and life and relationship coach. After twenty-seven years of professional and personal experience, Val sees a huge trend in today's society. This trend is that people want to have successful relationships in their professional and personal lives but they simply don't know how to get there. Val is here to help us solve this problem. Practice her *Nine Crucial Connection Keys* and the result will be a happier, more productive, and less stressed-out you that leads to greater success in all areas of your life.

Val combines her wealth of knowledge and techniques to help organizations boost people skills, build self-confidence, enhance communication, and strengthen relationships for remarkable results.

Val Baldwin, welcome to *Speaking of Success.*

Val Baldwin, CPC (Baldwin)

Thank you, David, I'm happy to be here.

Wright

What do our readers need to think about first to start improving their relationships and are these concepts applicable to both personal and professional relationships?

Baldwin

Absolutely. These concepts are universal and can be used with all the people in your life. We're not born knowing how to have successful relationships. Most of us just shoot from the hip with lousy results. Organizations falter and personal relationships crumble because of poor people skills.

The good news is that research has told us a great deal about what it takes to strengthen relationships with our family members, friends, and coworkers. It takes skills—relationship skills—and the even better news is that these skills can be learned. Does it take effort, patience, and practice? Yes. But I promise you it's worth every ounce of effort you put into it.

Before I explain the Nine Crucial Connection Keys I want you to think about the most difficult person you encounter. I've got four questions I want you to think about. You can write them down or think about them in your head.

As specifically as you can, think through what makes this relationship difficult for you. Write down four things that if they happened would repair the relationship. Of these four things, how many of them have the other person changing? For example, you might think, "If only that person would do this" or "If they would stop doing that . . ." or whatever the case may be.

Think about those four things and how many of them have the other person changing and how many of those four things have you doing the changing? If the majority of those four things have the other person changing, you need to look at yourself and see what part you play in making the relationship difficult. The truth is (and a lot of us don't like to hear this) you are the only one you can change. And you can't change what you don't first acknowledge. Most of us are clueless about how we come across to others. Although it's absolutely true that there are times when we are mere bystanders in a tough relationship, rarely are we completely innocent. More often than not we do something to contribute to the problems we're experiencing. Although we can't change the other person, by changing our own behavior toward another person in a more positive way, chances are that he or she will treat us better as well.

These connection keys are not rocket science. We know we should be doing them but most of us need a little reminder from time to time to get back on track and start moving in the right direction. Some connection keys will come easily to you and others will not.

As I talk about each key, I want you to rate yourself between a one and ten to see which keys you're already doing great and which ones could use improvement. If you rate yourself an eight to ten, you're really on top of it—it comes easy to you. If you rate yourself a one to three, you have a lot of work to do. After you rate yourself, have someone else who knows you very well take a look at your scores. This person might have a different opinion about how you interact with others. Please listen with an open mind and honestly consider his or her feedback.

Wright

Tell our readers about connection key number one: "Walk the talk."

Baldwin

When you "Walk the talk" you are being a person of integrity. Integrity means being honest, trustworthy, and doing what you say you will do, no matter what. Trust is the number one characteristic that is the hardest to rebuild once it's lost. If you choose just one key to commit to and you rated yourself low here, start with this one—it is the most important.

I speak to a wide variety of corporations, organizations, and groups. They tell me that one of the biggest problems is the lack of integrity in people today. Corporations crumble (we all know what happened to Enron), friendships are lost, and marriages are destroyed when trust is lost. It's a huge problem in our society. Individuals with high integrity are considered priceless in any organization or family.

Some people think integrity is not important or it's old-fashioned. People whose main purpose is going after the almighty dollar will rationalize their dishonest behavior in the workplace. People who are self-absorbed will rationalize their unreliable or dishonest behavior saying they are just fulfilling their own needs.

Choose to be the kind of person people can depend on to be true to your word. Think of people you've worked with or members of your family who you feel have high integrity. How do you regard them? What are some of the words and feelings that come to mind when you think about them? Are you grateful and relieved that that highly responsible person is on your team for the new project at work? Are you ecstatic that your Uncle John is helping you organize the family reunion this year because he is a man you can trust and will come through on what he says he will do? Most of us are excited to have people of high integrity with us to work on something together. You should want people to think that about you.

Think about words and feelings that come to mind when you're asked to be involved in something with people of low integrity. You think they're flaky and unreliable; it takes more time to baby-sit them to make sure they are doing their part than to just handle it yourself. You can see the obvious difference. Integrity is that powerful.

If you're assigned to work with someone on a project, what feelings do the others have about you? Would they be thinking it's great—you do what you say you will do? Or would they feel differently? Can they trust you to do what you say? Are you the kind of person they are excited to have on their team?

I've interviewed numerous employees about the value of integrity. A whopping 95 percent said they would prefer working for managers who are jerks—who are abrasive—but who they can trust and depend on to do what they say they will do versus a charming, kind manager who they can't depend on or trust.

Integrity is a priceless characteristic and you will be treated with honor and respect because of it. "Walk the talk" and show integrity in your words, actions, and deeds. Establish high integrity and you *will* have success in life.

Wright

Key number two is, "Say less than you think," which could be difficult for those of us who are paid to give advice. In what situations should we follow this key?

Baldwin

I'll be the first to admit that this is the hardest connection key for me to follow. What this means is we have to learn to zip our lip sometimes. Get the duct tape out if necessary. Many people like to hear themselves talk and always get their opinion in but quite often we say too much—especially those of us who get paid to tell others what we think. It's just our natural inclination but it's not always appropriate. Think twice before you open your mouth and spill out everything that's on your mind. This is especially true for close family members where we just usually say immediately what comes into our head. That's not the best technique to use to connect with others.

We're usually pretty good at work—we keep those boundaries up. Most of us rarely come out of a staff meeting and say something like, "Joe, what were you thinking? That was an idiotic presentation!" Most of us don't do that; we keep our boundaries up and show respect but at home we're not always so good.

Before you say whatever pops into your head, think about this: What do I really want for this relationship? How should I behave to get those results? If you're not behaving in a way that will get them then alter your behavior so you will get those results. Maybe it means saying less than you think.

Let me give you an example of when I really blew it. I have two children. I have a twenty-three-year-old son and a twenty-year-old daughter. I learned the importance of this key when my son came home after spending two years in Chile doing community service and missionary work from the ages of nineteen to twenty-one. Let me give you some background. Nick is a great kid but in high school, like most boys his age, he wasn't exactly "Mr. Motivated." His priorities were his friends, sports, and girls. He worked just enough to get decent grades but I had to do a lot of prodding and supervising (he would call it nagging and bugging) to keep him on track. When he came home after his life-enhancing experience in Chile, I still thought of him as the kid he was before he left. I was accustomed to the teenage Nick and not the new and improved twenty-one-year-old adult.

Nick returned home a few months before the next college semester started, so his main goal was to get a job. As his parent, by golly, I was going to jump in to help him succeed! Every day I would prod him and say, "Hey Nick, did you see that so-and-so is hiring?" or "Have you called back on that interview yet?" or "Do you want me to call Uncle Bob to see if he's hiring right now?" I stepped right back into my supervising mother role saying every thought that popped into my head.

After a week he finally said to me, "Mom, I know you are trying to help me but you are driving me crazy! I can do this myself. You've got to back off! Believe it or not, I somehow managed just fine without you for those two years in Chile. I'm twenty-one and I don't need my mother to get me a job. And besides, as a life coach, don't you teach people that you can learn life's biggest lessons through your biggest challenges? You have to let me fail."

He was absolutely right. As parents we sometimes become what I call "helicopter parents"—we're hovering around them all the time so they can't possibly fail. But sometimes failure is exactly what they need to experience. How else will they learn for themselves what it takes to be successful?

Tie this back to the question of "what do I want for this relationship?" The answer to that would be, "I want a loving, open, respectful relationship with my son." I'm sure I'm no different from other parents when I say my main objective is to raise a self-sufficient, independent adult who can provide for himself in the world. The question is how am I behaving? Was I behaving in a way that produces those results? Absolutely not! I needed to back off, change my behavior, and let him act like an adult. That's why, when I'm dealing with my two adult kids I need to learn to say less than I think to get the result that I want. With adult children we need to be their consultants—not their managers. Offer advice only when they come to us and ask.

This applies to the business world as well. If you want responsible, self-sufficient employees, are you always micro-managing and telling them every detail of what to do? If so, step back, adjust your behavior, and keep your end goal in mind.

If you're in a disagreement with your mother-in-law, when the conversation starts to heat up, stop and think about what you really want for this relationship and how you should behave to get those results. If you want a loving relationship with your mother-in-law, maybe you don't need to be right on this particular issue. Maybe you should back off, say less than you think, and simply let it go.

When I think of my own struggle to consciously apply this connection key, I think of one of my favorite quotes from the movie *Million Dollar Baby.* It says, "Have you ever noticed that the hardest thing to do and the right thing to do is usually the same thing?" How true!

Wright

So what do you mean by key number three: "Follow the 'Five-to-One Ratio'"?

Baldwin

I love this one. Psychologist Dr. John Gottman is a brilliant therapist at the University of Washington. Gottman and his colleagues conducted twenty years of research observing couples in his "Love Lab." He would videotape couples as they interact. He watched them talk. He watched them fight. He would hook them up to all these gadgets to see what their heart rate was and their pulse and how much they would fidget around in their chairs. Dr. Gottman is so good that he can predict with 94 percent accuracy whether a particular couple will stay together or not.

One of the results that came out of his twenty-year study was the Five-to-One Ratio. What this means is that it takes five positive things—compliments, encouraging words, acts—to offset every one negative. Basically, couples who stay together are nice to each other more often than not. They have maintained a five-to-one ratio of positive to negative moments without even realizing what they were doing. That's the power and that's the poison of negativity. For children the ratio is more like ten to one. When I first read this I thought, "Oh my gosh, I'm a horrible person, I'm certainly not doing that, especially not with my kids." I realized I needed to do more of this—I needed to give more compliments and to use more encouraging words.

I use this regularly in my speaking career and in my coaching practice—I give people what I call "The Val Gal Challenge." If you think something positive about someone, say it out loud. If you can't think of anything positive, think harder! Let's say you've done a presentation and you felt really great about it. You received numerous positive comments but you received one negative comment. What comment will you remember the most? The negative comment will stay with you. That's the poison of negativity.

I don't care if it involves people you know or strangers, give sincere compliments out freely. Compliment the grocery store check-out clerk at how efficient he or she is. Thank the waitress or waiter at how much you enjoyed the service you received. Compliment someone on his or her good-looking haircut or great outfit or your coworkers on their terrific presentation. Think about how many times you've thought something positive about someone but didn't bother sharing it with him or her. It's time to speak up and make someone's day. It may be the only compliment that person has received in a long time.

Now you know the incredible power and influence of the positive. Following the Five-to-One Ratio makes others feel great, but watch what it does for you. It's amazing. I love it when I give compliments because I see people light up and I feel just as good as they do. It's a great feeling and it's the right way to live. If you want to build better connections, follow the Five-to-One Ratio and watch the positive changes begin.

Start with committing to give three positive comments a day. Even if you are shy, this connection key can soon become an easy habit. I started practicing this Five-to-One ratio several years ago. Now I literally cannot keep my mouth shut when I think something good about someone—no matter who it is. The compliment just jumps out of my mouth before I even think twice about it. I *have* to say it whether I know the person or not. What I have found is you will never offend anyone with a sincere compliment or a kind word. You'll also find that people will seek you out and want to be around you. Just imagine what a better planet this would be if we all followed the Five-to-One Ratio. Why not begin with you?

Wright

"You're not the only one," is key number four. Does this have to do with being self-centered?

Baldwin

You're absolutely right. Have you ever been around people who are self-absorbed and only talk about themselves? We all have and it can be incredibly draining. You begin to wonder why you are even in the room. It's not pleasant. To build stronger connections you must remember that you're not the only one here on the planet.

Here's a big clue: if you look around you and the person you're talking to starts to get a glazed look in his or her eyes, stop talking about yourself and start asking about the other person. Ask questions about his or her pursuits, work, home, and family. We can learn so much from others' life experiences. And when you focus on others it helps you forget about your own problems.

Let me give you a case in point. I had a client who was very high up on the corporate ladder in a health care organization. She is an amazing person. She really cared about her employees. She had just received her review and she was rated low. Her employees seemed to think she didn't care about them and she wasn't really interested in what they had to say or what they were involved with. She was mortified. They had gone through several cuts and she was literally doing two full-time jobs. She simply didn't have the time and was doing the best she could to keep things afloat.

We came up with an idea. We called it "The Monday Morning Rounds." It was to help her connect with her employees. What she would do every Monday morning from eight until nine o'clock was go around and make sure she connected with every single employee. They didn't know this was an assignment from her coach (me) but she did this with sincerity. She asked about them. She would say things like, "Hey Joe, great to see you this morning. How was your weekend?" "Sally, how did it go with your son's birthday party on Saturday?" "Hey Sam, I wanted to tell you again what a great job you did on the new budget proposal. Did you do anything fun this weekend?"

She asked about them—she looked them in the eye. She sincerely wanted to know how they were. She would give compliments, she would connect with them, and she would ask about them. She really wanted to know—she wanted to connect.

Six months later, when she got her next review, she was given an excellent rating because they felt valued. They felt that she cared about them. That made all the difference in the world.

Wright

I've heard of research done on the impact that positive personalities have in the workplace versus negative personalities. Is this what you're referring to with key number five—"The power of positive?

Baldwin

Yes, I am. This is not only true for the workplace but of course for our personal lives as well. It's amazing how easy it is for people who are cheerful and positive to build strong connections with others. Everybody likes being around them. Who likes being around a "Debbie Downer" or a "Negative Ned"? Those are people who always look to the negative and they're always in a grumpy mood. It's not fun to be around these people. I personally try to avoid them and limit my time with people who are this way. Sometimes we don't have a choice. Ask yourself and ask others who know you well if you come across as positive or negative. Is the glass half empty or is it half full for you?

When I present this topic at speaking engagements, I ask the audience members to raise their hands if they consider themselves to be a positive and cheerful person. It's fascinating to me that very few people consider themselves to be cheerful. But we all love being around someone who is.

Studies conducted at the Stanford University Psychology Department show that people are naturally drawn to people who are cheerful and have a positive look on their face. You will actually get better service and a better response at restaurants, banks, and from coworkers, family, and friends no matter where you are and what you're doing if you are cheerful.

Being positive and cheerful may sound like a really simple thing to do but it's not easy for a lot of people. It takes conscious effort to change our natural reaction to life and the world around us when we are set in a negative pattern, but you can do it.

Here's how it works. Our brain has three-quarters of a second to choose how we will react to something. If we are always reacting negatively it's easiest for our brain to go automatically down that negative path. Three-quarters of a second, though, is plenty of time to consciously stop yourself, readjust, and choose to react positively. Once you begin to choose to react positively, that will also become a habit and your brain will adjust to automatically go down the positive path. It takes time and conscious effort to reprogram your automatic thought process, but it is absolutely doable.

I had a client who told me about his company's customer service group. They were always looking for ways to increase their customer service phone support. They had recently been reviewed and it was bad. They decided to put mirrors inside each of the representatives' workstations and told them to smile while answering the phone. The result was amazing. First of all they were laughing at themselves because they felt goofy watching themselves smile in the mirror. The end result was they came across more positive, their attitude toward the callers improved, and the next time they underwent the review process they received a good rating. Simply putting a smile on their faces created a positive attitude and they handled the callers' issues in a much more constructive way.

I tell singles I work with who want more dates to get out of the house and do one thing a week that they love to do. The result is that they will meet more people, they will be smiling more often, and that will make them more attractive to others.

Having a happy personality is not magical—it takes effort. But once you start pushing yourself to do things like answering the phone with a bright, "Hello!" or smiling at the receptionist or the security guard when you get to work in the morning or greeting your family members with a smile when you see them will become more automatic.

One more secret to this is to take on an attitude of gratitude. Your subconscious mind cannot process fear (which produces anger) and gratitude at the same time. It can switch back and forth but when you have an attitude of gratefulness, you can't have anger or fear. What I suggest clients do—people who are very negative—is have them start a gratitude journal. First thing in the morning or last thing at night, write down three simple things that you're grateful for. It can be simple things like it was a beautiful fall day with the leaves turning colors or you petted an adorable little puppy or you got along with your difficult co-worker today. By writing down what you're grateful for you'll have a heart and brain filled with gratitude; you cannot have anger or fear at the same time.

For people who are extremely negative I have them do this exercise three times a day to keep the anger and fear under control. Soon their positive side takes over. Try it. It works like magic.

Wright

Tell me about key number six—"Your mind: open or closed?"

Baldwin

Have you ever worked for or with someone who is extremely closed-minded? Maybe you have family members who are this way. Do you feel open to suggesting new ideas to these kinds of people? Heck no. If we perceive that someone is closed-minded most of us think why bother, he (or she) won't listen anyway. It is a mark of a superior mind to be able to disagree without being disagreeable. Always show respect and openness for others' opinions, whether you agree or not. Just remember that no one is right every single time. We've all met people who think they are, but it's impossible to be right 100 percent of the time.

If you have ten different people witness the same event, they will come up with ten different accounts of that same event. They are all right but they just experience it in their own unique way.

Being open-minded is a wonderful way to create closeness and connection with others. People will want to talk with you. People will feel safe to approach you with their ideas because of this characteristic. The best communicators show their open-mindedness in all their dealings. This rings true in families, groups, and in the business world.

Your organization will be much more effective and productive if all members feel it's safe to bring their views and ideas to the table. You may be the one who makes the final decision, but the best results come from the more ideas you have to consider. If people view you as judgmental and closed-minded they will hold back, which will cause brilliant solutions and ideas to go unheard. Fear will always keep people quiet.

Here's an example that shows openness. Remember to say these things with sincerity—that's what counts. Let's say you've been working on a new project and you're really excited to present this to your team. You feel great about it but you also know that you want their honest feedback. You want this project to be successful, not only for you but also for everyone in your group. To show open-mindedness, at the end of your presentation make comments like this: "Am I missing anything with this proposal? I really want to know what you think. Certainly I don't know everything and I don't want to overlook anything, so I would really like to hear your ideas." Or you can say, "I know we all want to come up with the very best solution, so let me know if there are other ways you can think of to address this." If you say something like this there won't be anyone in that room who wouldn't feel comfortable in offering other ideas and suggestions. That is open-mindedness. But don't just say the words and then immediately shut down any feedback. Truly accept and consider others' ideas. You will have more success with all the people in your life if you follow this key.

Wright

You've peaked my curiosity about the connection key number seven. What does the "G" word mean?

Baldwin

Ah, the "G" word. The "G" word refers to gossip. Be careful of others' feelings and refuse to talk about another's vices. Gossip is poison in any relationship and it's poison in professional organizations as well.

I get requests to speak to groups where this is a huge problem. These organizations are less productive and have higher turnover because no one wants to be involved in a group whose members tear each other down. When there's a drama going on every day it takes valuable time and energy away from what people are supposed to be doing. I'm sure you've experienced this and know how damaging it can be. It's equally as disastrous with groups of friends and family members.

Let me tell you what is actually happening with people who tend to gossip a lot. I'm very fortunate because I've been happily married to the love of my life for twenty-seven years. He is a neuropsychologist so you can imagine the crazy conversations at our house between a life coach (me) and a neuropsychologist! The cool part is that he shares with me really fascinating information about the power of the brain and what really causes so many people's problems. What we both find to be true is that most people who gossip regularly about others actually have low self-esteem themselves. Yes, a very small number of people who continually gossip are self-centered and they think they're God's gift to the universe; but typically, more often than not, these people have low self-esteem. They tear down others to try and make themselves feel better and actually, the opposite happens—they just don't know it.

Studies prove that when you verbally tear someone down, your subconscious mind cannot tell the difference between you saying it about someone else or saying it about yourself. That is why most of us get this bad feeling in our gut after we've said something negative about someone else. Your subconscious mind perceives you just said it about yourself as well. The unfortunate result is that people continue to gossip about others to help themselves feel better, but in reality they're tearing themselves down time and time again. They are unknowingly putting themselves in a continual downward spiral of self-destruction.

If you catch yourself gossiping, notice how you feel. You will stop because you now understand that the ultimate outcome is a negative result for you.

There are two ways to stop gossip. If you're in a situation at work with friends or relatives or whatever the circumstances may be, both methods work. The first one is the easiest. All you have to do when someone begins to gossip is to simply, in a polite way, excuse yourself and leave. You might have to make a phone call, or perhaps you have a meeting to get to, etc. Remove yourself from the situation.

The second is a little more difficult but much more powerful. Let's say someone is gossiping about Sally. What you can do is not to tear down the person for gossiping about Sally, you simply say something positive about Sally. That will stop the gossip in its tracks. For example you could say, "I know you think Sally is kind of crazy but I saw her with her daughter last week and she is an amazing parent. I wish you could have seen her." You can continue on to say a couple of positive things about her. Most people will stop the negative talk. You didn't insult the person who was gossiping, but you have turned the conversation from being negative into being positive.

Now that you understand what is really happening in your brain when you gossip, hopefully you will never get caught up in this poisonous behavior again.

Wright

"Letting it go" is key number eight. What should we let go?

Baldwin

When someone does something that annoys you, you need to keep your anger and defensiveness down. Connection key number eight is to pay no attention to negative remarks that are said about you. Learn to blow it off—learn to let it go. Yes, it can hurt. Yes, you might wonder why someone said something negative about you. Yes, your natural reaction is to strike back, but don't. Don't waste your time and energy on this kind of behavior. Learn to "turn the other cheek."

The thing is this: you don't know what is going on inside the head of someone who is acting in this negative way. The person might be having a bad day or have received bad news about his or her job or had a fight with a child or spouse. People may have low self-esteem and feel they need to cut you down in order to make themselves look better. You just don't know what's going on in their life that may have caused them to behave as they did.

To help yourself calm down and react in a mature manner, ask yourself what I call the softening question: why would a rational, reasonable adult act like this? When you ask that question it will soften your heart toward that person. It will help you understand that person's point of view, which will tear down your defensiveness and the anger you may naturally feel toward him or her.

Let me tell you a story about a friend and her coworker. We'll call my friend Sarah. Sarah got a new job involving job-sharing at a medical office with Jill. Jill had been there for several years; she had requested to move from full-time to part-time. Sarah was hired to job-share with her. They were both happy with the situation. My friend, Sarah, soon found out that Jill was gossiping about her to all the other staff and doctors on days she was not there. Sarah was understandably upset and couldn't understand why Jill would do this, especially since Sarah was highly competent, very experienced, and was doing a great job. Sarah was the very reason Jill could move to part-time. Sarah got extremely angry. She wanted to strike back at Jill. The situation made her new job-share experience horrible. She hated going to work because she would hear what Jill had said about her. Even though Sarah loved the job itself and the other employees, the anger and pain she was feeling about the gossip caused her to consider quitting.

I asked my friend, Sarah, to learn more about Jill as a person and find out what her background was. I asked Sarah to ask herself this softening question: why would a rational, reasonable adult act this way? What Sarah found out was that Jill had a very difficult, troubled relationship at home. She had been verbally abused, she rarely felt good about anything in her life, and this job was the only place where she felt valued and special. The doctors liked her, her coworkers liked her, and she felt she had an amazing connection with everyone at work. Now that she was sharing her position with Sarah, Jill felt threatened and insecure. She wanted to make sure she could still be the "queen bee" of the office and she didn't want to share her close association with the boss.

That was the reason Jill was gossiping. Does that make it right? Absolutely not. But my friend, Sarah, could then understand where Jill was coming from. She didn't like it but she understood it. Sarah could then let go of her anger and resentment and she no longer felt like attacking Jill—she felt compassion for her. Now Sarah could have a mature and rational conversation with Jill about how they could make the situation work for both of them. Asking the softening question changed Sarah's attitude completely.

The simple secret—the real secret—of letting go of negative remarks said about you is this: live your life in a way that nobody will believe them.

Wright

The final key is "Don't wait for credit due you." Why is this an imortant key to follow?

Baldwin

If you are choosing to do good deeds simply because you want to get credit from others, you are going to be waiting a very long time and you will be disappointed. You should do good deeds and perform at your best, not to get kudos from the world but to please yourself and because you know it's the right thing to do. Forget about yourself and let others remember. Success is much sweeter that way.

Wright

So do you have any final thoughts to help our readers build healthier, successful relationships?

Baldwin

I do. Readers, take a look at your list. How did you do? Hopefully you were rating yourself one through ten on all of these crucial connection keys. Maybe there were some surprises. Again, take your list to someone who knows you very, very well and see if that person agrees with your rating. Maybe you're better in some areas than you think you are or maybe you're not as good in some areas as you think you are. It's easy for us to be clueless about our own behavior. You can't change what you don't first acknowledge. Seeing the areas where you need improvement is a good thing—it's the very first step in making better connections with others. Knowledge is first. Taking action is second.

To have success in your life you need to understand that people matter most. Ask yourself this: when you're ninety-nine and looking back at your life, will it be the *things* you've acquired or your strong *people connections* that gave your life meaning and fulfillment?

It's never too late to make better connections with others. The trick is realizing that the only person you can change is yourself. Start here—start now. Commit to just one of these connection keys and practice it over and over until it becomes a part of you. Then take on another one and then another. You *can* do it. Will it take effort, time, and patience? Absolutely. But I promise you, the results will be priceless.

My parting comment is that I wish you all incredible lives. Now go get started!

Wright

Today we've been talking with Val Baldwin. Val is a professional speaker, trainer, and life and relationship coach. As we've found here, I think she knows what she's talking about—at least, she's teaching me!

Thank you so much, Val, for being with us on *Speaking of Success.*

About the Author

To VAL BALDWIN, *people* matter most. The minute you meet her, you feel you know her and connect immediately. Her husband lovingly calls her the "human can-opener." In a matter of minutes, you find yourself sharing things you never thought you would.

In fact, the first time she appeared on Portland television, the executive producer told her she had a rare, transparent quality, being exactly the same person on or off camera. They loved her dynamic enthusiasm and spunky attitude and invited Val to be a regular on their show.

Educated in business and psychology, Val spent twenty-three years in the corporate world in marketing, customer service, and training. She experienced first-hand the difference in individuals who had effective people skills and those who didn't.

Val soon developed a desire to help people gain these skills to improve their lives and relationships. She went back to school and became certified in Life and Relationship Coaching and set up her private coaching practice to do just that.

Now, as a professional speaker, Val combines her wealth of knowledge and techniques to help organizations boost people skills, build self-confidence, enhance communication, and strengthen relationships.

Val has been happily married to her neuropsychologist husband, Matt, for over twenty-seven years and they have two beloved children. The most telling quote you'll hear Val say is, "After twenty-seven years, my man still takes my breath away!" Val loves her work and feels it's her mission to help people get the skills to make their lives and relationships remarkable.

Val Baldwin, CPC
Live Your Ultimate Life NOW!
Portland, OR 97006
Phone: 503.473.7901
E-mail: info@valbaldwin.com
www.valbaldwin.com
—Helping people get along for greater success in life—

Chapter 7

DR. STEPHEN R. COVEY

David Wright (Wright)

We're talking today with Dr. Stephen R. Covey, cofounder and vice-chairman of Franklin Covey Company, the largest management company and leadership development organization in the world. Dr. Covey is perhaps best known as the author of *The 7 Habits of Highly Effective People* which is ranked as a number one best seller by the *New York Times*, having sold more than fourteen million copies in thirty-eight languages throughout the world. Dr. Covey is an internationally respected leadership authority, family expert, teacher, and organizational consultant. He has made teaching principle-centered living and principle-centered leadership his life's work. Dr. Covey is the recipient of the Thomas More College Medallion for Continuing Service to Humanity and has been awarded four honorary doctorate degrees. Other awards given Dr. Covey include the Sikh's 1989 International Man of Peace award, the 1994 International Entrepreneur of the Year award, *Inc. magazine's* Services Entrepreneur of the Year award, and in 1996 the National Entrepreneur of the Year Lifetime Achievement award for Entrepreneurial leadership. He has also been recognized as one of *Time Magazine's* twenty-five most influential Americans and one of Sales and Marketing Management's top twenty-five power brokers. Dr. Covey earned his undergraduate degree from the University of Utah, his MBA from Harvard, and completed his doctorate at Brigham Young University. While at Brigham Young he served as assistant to the President and was also a professor of business management and organizational behavior. Dr. Covey, welcome to *Speaking of Success!*

Dr. Stephen Covey (Covey)

Thank you.

Wright

Dr. Covey, most companies make decisions and filter them down through their organization. You, however, state that no company can succeed until individuals within it succeed. Are the goals of the company the result of the combined goals of the individuals?

Covey

Absolutely, because if people aren't on the same page they're going to be pulling in different directions. To teach this concept, I frequently ask large audiences to close their eyes and point north, and then to keep pointing and open their eyes and they find themselves pointing all over the place. I say to them, "Tomorrow morning if you want a similar experience, ask the first ten people you meet in your organization what the purpose of your organization is and you'll find it's a very similar experience. They'll point all over the place." When people have a different sense of purpose and values, every decision that is made from then on is governed by those. There's no question that this is one of the fundamental causes of misalignment, low trust, interpersonal conflict, interdepartmental rivalry, people operating on personal agendas, and so forth.

Wright

Is that mostly a result of the inability to communicate from the top?

Covey

That's one aspect, but I think it's more fundamental. There's an inability to involve people—an unwillingness. Leaders may communicate what their mission and their strategy is, but that doesn't mean there's any emotional connection to it. Mission statements that are rushed and then announced are soon forgotten. They become nothing more than just a bunch of platitudes on the wall that mean essentially nothing and even create a source of cynicism and a sense of hypocrisy inside the culture of an organization.

Wright

How do companies ensure survival and prosperity in these tumultuous times of technological advances, mergers, downsizing, and change?

Covey

I think that it takes a lot of high trust in a culture that has something that doesn't change—principles—at its core. There are principles that people agree upon that are valued. It gives a sense of stability. Then you have the power to adapt and be flexible when you experience these kinds of disruptive new economic models or technologies that come in and sideswipe you. You don't know how to handle them unless you have something you can depend upon. If people have not agreed to a common set of principles that guide them and a common purpose, then they get their security from the outside and they tend to freeze the structure, systems, and processes inside and they cease becoming adaptable. They don't change with the changing realities of the new marketplace out there and gradually they become obsolete.

Wright

I was interested in one portion of your book *The 7 Habits of Highly Effective People* where you talk about behaviors. How does an individual go about the process of replacing ineffective behaviors with effective ones?

Covey

I think that for most people it usually requires a crisis that humbles them to become aware of their ineffective behaviors. If there's not a crisis the tendency is to perpetuate those behaviors and not change. You don't have to wait until the marketplace creates the crisis for you. Have everyone accountable on a 360 degree basis to everyone else they interact with—with feedback either formal or informal—where they are getting data as to what's happening. They will then start to realize that the consequences of their ineffective behavior require them to be humble enough to look at that behavior and to adopt new, more effective ways of doing things. Sometimes people can be stirred up to this if you just appeal to their conscience—to their inward sense of what is right and wrong. A lot of people sometimes know inwardly they're doing wrong, but the culture doesn't necessarily discourage them from continuing that. They either need feedback from people, or they need feedback from the marketplace, or they need feedback from their conscience. Then they can begin to develop a step-by-step process of replacing old habits with new, better habits.

Wright

It's almost like saying, "Let's make all the mistakes in the laboratory before we put this thing in the air."

Covey

Right; and I also think what is necessary is a paradigm shift, which is analogous to having a correct map, say of a city or of a country. If people have an inaccurate paradigm of life, of other people, and of themselves it really doesn't make much difference what their behavior or habits or attitudes are. What they need is a correct paradigm—a correct map—that describes what's going on. For instance, in the Middle Ages they used to heal people through bloodletting. It wasn't until Samuel Weiss and Pasteur and other empirical scientists discovered the germ theory that they realized for the first time they weren't dealing with the real issue. They realized why women preferred to use midwives who washed rather than doctors who didn't wash. They gradually got a new paradigm. Once you've got a new paradigm then your behavior and your attitude flows directly from it. If you have a bad paradigm or a bad map, let's say of a city, there's no way, no matter what your behavior or your habits or your attitudes are—how positive they are—you'll never be able to find the location you're looking for. This is why I believe that to change paradigms is far more fundamental than to work on attitude and behavior.

Wright

One of your seven habits of highly effective people is to begin with the end in mind. If circumstances change and hardships or miscalculation occurs, how does one view the end with clarity?

Covey

Many people think to begin with the end in mind means that you have some fixed definition of a goal that's accomplished and if changes come about you're not going to adapt to them. Instead, the "end in mind" you begin with is that you are going to create a flexible culture of high trust so that no matter what comes along you are going to do whatever it takes to accommodate that new change or that new reality and maintain a culture of high performance and high trust. You're talking more in terms of values and overall purposes which don't change, rather than specific strategies or programs that will have to change to accommodate the changing realities in the marketplace.

Wright

In this time of mistrust between people, corporations, and nations for that matter, how do we create high levels of trust?

Covey

That's a great question and it's complicated because there are so many elements that go into the creating of a culture of trust. Obviously the most fundamental one is just to have trustworthy people. But that is not sufficient because what if the organization itself is misaligned? For instance, what if you say you value cooperation but you really reward people for internal competition? Then you have a systemic or a structure problem that creates low trust inside the culture even though the people themselves are trustworthy. This is one of the insights of Edward Demming and the work he did. That's why he said that most problems are not personal; they're systemic. They're common caused. That's why you have to work on structure, systems, and processes to make sure that they institutionalize principle-centered values. Otherwise you could have good people with bad systems and you'll get bad results.

When it comes to developing interpersonal trust between people, it is made up of many, many elements such as taking the time to listen to other people, to understand them, and to see what is important to them. What we think is important to another may only be important to us, not to another. It takes empathy. You have to make and keep promises to them. You have to treat them with kindness and courtesy. You have to be completely honest and open. You have to live up to your commitments. You can't betray them behind their back. You can't badmouth them behind their back and sweet-talk them to their face. That will send out vibes of hypocrisy and it will be detected. You have to learn to apologize when you make mistakes, to admit mistakes, and to also get feedback going in every direction as much as possible. It doesn't necessarily require formal forums; it requires trust between people that will be open with each other and give each other feedback.

Wright

My mother told me to do a lot of what you're saying now, but it seems like when I got in business I simply forgot.

Covey

Sometimes we forget, but sometimes culture doesn't nurture it. That's why I say unless you work with the institutionalizing—that means formalizing into structure, systems, and processes the values—you will not have a nurturing culture. You have to constantly work on that. This is one of the big mistakes organizations make. They think trust is simply a function of being honest. That's only one small aspect. It's an important aspect, obviously, but there are so many other elements that go into the creation of a high trust culture.

Wright

"Seek first to understand then to be understood" is another of your seven habits. Do you find that people try to communicate without really understanding what other people want?

Covey

Absolutely. The tendency is to project out of our own autobiography—our own life, our own value system—onto other people, thinking we know what they want. So we don't really listen to them. We pretend to listen, but we really don't listen from within their frame of reference. We listen from within our own frame of reference and we're really preparing our reply rather than seeking to understand. This is a very common thing. In fact very few people have had any training in seriously listening. They're trained in how to read, write, and speak, but not to listen.

Reading, writing, speaking, and listening are the four modes of communication and they represent about two-thirds to three-fourths of our waking hours. About half of that time is spent listening, but it's the one skill people have not been trained in. People have had all this training in the other forms of communication. In a large audience of

1,000 people you wouldn't have more than twenty people who have had more than two weeks of training in listening. Listening is more than a skill or a technique so that you're listening within another frame of reference. It takes tremendous courage to listen because you're at risk when you listen. You don't know what's going to happen; you're vulnerable.

Wright

Sales gurus always tell me that the number one skill in selling is listening.

Covey

Yes—listening from within the customer's frame of reference. That is so true. You can see that it takes some security to do that because you don't know what's going to happen.

Wright

With our *Speaking of Success!* talk show and book we're trying to encourage people in our audience to be better, to live better, and be more fulfilled by listening to the examples of our guests. Is there anything or anyone in your life that has made a difference for you and helped you to become a better person?

Covey

I think the most influential people in my life have been my parents. I think that what they modeled was not to make comparisons and harbor jealousy or to seek recognition. They were humble people. I remember my mother one time when we were going up in an elevator and the most prominent person in the state was in the elevator. She knew him, but she spent her time talking to the elevator operator. I was just a little kid and I was so awed by this person and I said to my mom, "Why didn't you talk to the important person?" She said, "I was. I had never met him." They were really humble, modest people who were focused on service and other people rather than on themselves. I think they were very inspiring models to me.

Wright

In almost every research paper that anyone I've ever read writes about people who influenced their lives, in the top five people, three of them are teachers. My seventh grade English teacher was the greatest teacher I ever had and influenced me to no end.

Covey

Would it be correct to say that she saw in you probably some qualities of greatness you didn't even see in yourself?

Wright

Absolutely.

Covey

That's been my general experience that the key aspect of a mentor or a teacher is someone who sees in you potential that you don't even see in yourself. They treat you accordingly and eventually you come to see it in yourself. That's my definition of leadership or influence—communicating people's worth and potential so clearly that they are inspired to see it in themselves.

Wright

Most of my teachers treated me as a student, but she treated me with much more respect than that. As a matter of fact, she called me Mr. Wright in the seventh grade. I'd never been addressed by anything but a nickname. I stood a little taller; she just made a tremendous difference. Do you think there are other characteristics that mentors seem to have in common?

Covey

I think they are first of all good examples in their own personal lives. Their personal lives and their family lives are not all messed up—they come from a base of good character. They also are usually very confident and they take the time to do what your teacher did to you—to treat you with uncommon respect and courtesy.

They also, I think, explicitly teach principles rather than practices so that rules don't take the place of human judgment. You gradually come to have faith in your own judgment in making decisions because of the affirmation of such a mentor. Good mentors care about you—you can feel the sincerity of their caring. It's like the expression, "I don't care how much you know until I know how much you care."

Wright

Most people are fascinated with the new television shows about being a survivor. What has been the greatest comeback that you've made from adversity in your career or your life?

Covey

When I was in grade school I experienced a disease in my legs. It caused me to use crutches for a while. I tried to get off them fast and get back. The disease wasn't corrected yet so I went back on crutches for another year. The disease went to the other leg and I went on for another year. It essentially took me out of my favorite thing—athletics—and it took me more into being a student. So that was kind of a life-defining experience which at the time seemed very negative, but has proven to be the basis on which I've focused my life—being more of a learner.

Wright

Principle-centered learning is basically what you do that's different from anybody I've read or listened to.

Covey

The concept is embodied in the far-eastern expression, "Give a man a fish, you feed him for the day; teach him how to fish, you feed him for a lifetime." When you teach principles that are universal and timeless, they don't belong to just any one person's religion or to a particular culture or geography. They seem to be timeless and universal like the ones we've been talking about here: trustworthiness, honesty, caring, service, growth, and development. These are universal principles. If you focus on these things then little by little people become independent of you and then they start to believe in themselves and their own judgment becomes better. You don't need as many rules. You don't need as much bureaucracy and as many controls and you can empower people.

The problem in most business operations today—and not just business but non-business—is that they're using the industrial model in an information age. Arnold Toynbee, the great historian, said, "You can pretty well summarize all of history in four words: nothing fails like success." The industrial model was based on the asset of the machine. The information model is based on the asset of the person—the knowledge worker. It's an altogether different model. But the machine model was the main asset of the twentieth century. It enabled productivity to increase fifty times. The new asset is intellectual and social capital—the qualities of people and the quality of the relationship they have with each other. Like Toynbee said, "Nothing fails like success." The industrial model does not work in an information age. It requires a focus on the new wealth, not capital and material things.

A good illustration that demonstrates how much we were into the industrial model, and still are, is to notice where people are on the balance sheet. They're not found there. Machines are found there. Machines become investments. People are on the profit and loss statement and people are expenses. Think of that; if that isn't blood-letting.

Wright

It sure is.

When you consider the choices you've made down through the years, has faith played an important role in your life?

Covey

It has played an extremely important role. I believe deeply that we should put principles at the center of our lives, but I believe that God is the source of those principles. I did not invent them. I get credit sometimes for some of the Seven Habits material and some of the other things I've done, but it's really all based on principles that have been given by God to all of His children from the beginning of time. You'll find that you can teach these same principles from the sacred texts and the wisdom literature of almost any tradition. I think the ultimate source of that is God and that is one thing you can absolutely depend upon—in God we trust.

Wright

If you could have a platform and tell our audience something you feel would help them or encourage them, what would you say?

Covey

I think I would say to put God at the center of your life and then prioritize your family. No one on their deathbed ever wished they spent more time at the office.

Wright

That's right. We have come down to the end of our program and I know you're a busy person, but I could talk with you all day Dr. Covey.

Covey

It's good to talk with you as well and to be a part of this program. It looks like an excellent one that you've got going on here.

Wright

Thank you.

We have been talking today with Dr. Stephen R. Covey, co-founder and vice-chairman of Franklin Covey Company. He's also the author of *The 7 Habits of Highly Effective People,* which has been ranked as a number one bestseller by the *New York Times*, selling more than fourteen million copies in thirty-eight languages.

Dr. Covey, thank you so much for being with us today on *Speaking of Success!*

Covey

Thank you for the honor of participating.

About The Author

In 1996, Stephen R. Covey was recognized as one of Time magazine's twenty-five most influential Americans and one of Sales and Marketing Management's top twenty-five power brokers. Dr. Covey is the author of several acclaimed books, including the international bestseller, *The 7 Habits of Highly Effective People*. It has sold more than fifteen million copies in thirty-eight languages throughout the world. Other bestsellers authored by Dr. Covey include *First Things First, Principle-Centered Leadership*, with sales exceeding one million, and *The 7 Habits of Highly Effective Families.*

Dr. Covey's newest book, *The 8th Habit: From Effectiveness to Greatness*, which was released in November 2004, has risen to the top of several bestseller lists, including *New York Times, Wall Street Journal, USA Today Money, Business Week*, and Amazon.com and Barnes & Noble. The 8th Habit has sold more than 360,000 copies.

Dr. Covey earned his undergraduate degree from the University of Utah, his MBA from Harvard, and completed his doctorate at Brigham Young University. While at Brigham Young University, he served as assistant to the president and was also a professor of business management and organizational behavior. He received the National Fatherhood Award in 2003, which, as the father of nine and grandfather of forty-four, he says is the most meaningful award he has ever received.

Dr. Covey currently serves on the board of directors for the Points of Light Foundation. Based in Washington, D.C., the Foundation, through its partnership with the Volunteer Center National Network, engages and mobilizes millions of volunteers from all walks of life—businesses, nonprofits, faith-based organizations, low-income communities, families, youth, and older adults—to help solve serious social problems in thousands of communities.

Dr. Stephen R. Covey
www.stephencovey.com

Chapter 8

DAVID A. ZIMMER

David Wright (Wright)

Today we are talking with David A. Zimmer, MSCS, CCP, founder of the American Eagle Group. Mr. Zimmer works with small to large companies to develop strategies that lead to their business success. He works with individuals using similar methods to develop plans for their success.

He earned his Master's Degree in Computer Science from Purdue University and a Master's Certificate in Project Management from Villanova University. He is a Certified Computing Professional.

Most importantly, he has developed a plan to help you achieve success. His step-by-step process breaks the road to success into manageable pieces. This plan has helped many become successful and he believes that it can help you as well.

David Zimmer, welcome to *Speaking of Success.*

David A. Zimmer (Zimmer)

Thank you, it's great to be here.

Wright

You have developed a tactical plan for success. What is a tactical plan for success?

Zimmer

A tactical plan provides the steps to achieve an objective. Using the dictionary definition, the term "tactical" has military overtones that describe a series of smaller steps that are used to achieve objectives. The tactical plan is not used long-term but rather it is used to support long-term goals.

The root word of tactical is *"tactics."* Let's look at the dictionary definition as displayed on *Answer.com:*

1.a. *(used with a singular verb)* The military science that deals with securing objectives set by strategy, especially the technique of deploying and directing troops, ships, and aircraft in effective maneuvers against an enemy:

1.b. *(used with a plural verb)* Maneuvers used against an enemy:

2. *(used with a singular or plural verb)* A procedure or set of maneuvers engaged in to achieve an end, an aim, or a goal.

We see that all three definitions fit nicely when it comes to a tactical plan for success. Our long-term strategy is to defeat the enemy of being unsuccessful; but we need a plan to achieve that goal. We need to deploy our "troops" (our skills and talents), our "ships" (desires), and "aircraft" (dreams) to meet our objective—the definition of success that we set for ourselves. Therefore, we must develop a plan—a tactical plan—that we can execute to achieve what we call success.

Wright

Hmm, interesting angle. I noticed that you subtly suggested a definition of success in your statement. How do you define success?

Zimmer

Success is defined by the individual. Success to one person may not be the same as it is to another person. And what many call success is not really success at all.

To many, success means gaining fame and fortune. But as I watch many of those who have obtained fame and fortune, many aspects of their lives are destroyed. In the news we often hear of those we consider successful who are battling alcoholism, eating disorders, drug abuse, unhappy marriages, suicide or attempted suicide, and other abnormal behaviors. It seems the pressure of maintaining the *success* is unbearable and they turn to other things they think will relieve them of that pressure. There are too many cases to ignore. There must be more to success than money and possessions. Or maybe the meaning of success is different. Is it simply meeting one's goals in life?

My conclusion is that success has to be something different. While it might include prosperity and notoriety, success must be something to experience without the negatives. I look around and see people who many would not consider "successful," and yet there is something about them that I would consider successful.

We have heard that *Success is the journey, not the end*, but somehow that left me wanting. I see those people who many consider successful and I see how they seem only to be successful in one area of life and not others; in fact, they are utter failures in those other areas. After much research and thinking, I have begun to really understand what success is. I have developed a methodology—a tactical plan—that when followed leads a person to a very satisfying and successful life. I have seen it evidenced in those peoples' lives who have followed it.

Success is not the clothes you wear, it is not the house you own, the car you drive, the money in your bank account, or the position you hold. Success is who you are. It comes from within. Determining who you are and who you want to become is the key.

So, putting it into a definition form: *success is being able to say at the end of one's life, "I have lived and I am happy with the result."* The definition leads to a multi-faceted approach and view of success.

My background has been managing projects for large and small companies. To manage a project I must have a system I can follow that takes the complex and boils it down to the simple. I have approached "being successful" in a similar manner by breaking it down into an actionable plan I can follow.

Wright

Will you share your plan with us? What is the first step in your plan?

Zimmer

My plan focuses on many areas of life. It is a very personal process and takes time to develop. I have the full plan template available on my Web site for free download (zimmerspeaks.com/successplan.html), but I will describe it here so that readers can get a flavor of the process.

Overall, the process takes a few hours, but a lifetime to complete. In fact, a person's plan evolves over time and changes as he or she completes goals and ages. As we complete some goals, we move on to new ones. Some goals are ongoing, never fully obtainable, such as *exercising three times a week*. That goal never ends and just because we don't exercise three times one week does not mean we are failures.

Which reminds me, in order to define success, we must also look at its opposite—failure. Just because I don't reach my goal or I don't succeed at a particular thing doesn't mean that I am a failure. Failure *only* occurs when I give up.

Thomas Edison didn't fail 9,999 times in creating the first successful lightbulb. He found 9,999 ways of not creating that lightbulb. Along the way he learned some valuable information that when pieced together resulted in success. He may have used the successful filament in experiment number 5,492 and another filament in a vacuum in experiment 8,329, but only by tracking his results was he able to combine the right ingredients to finally put the proper filament into a vacuum and watch it light the earth. So each "failure" provided important information for the next round. It is the same with our abilities to achieve goals.

With that said, we need to prepare for the exercise.

Preparation
1. Find a three- to four-hour time slot which will not be interrupted.
2. Find a quiet place with no distractions.
3. Use the free, downloaded Tactical Plan template, printed on paper.
4. Have pencils and erasers ready for the session.

First Step
The first step is to determine your values. Values determine how you view life. They are the ideas and thoughts that govern your well-being. Basically, you operate by your values. Once these are established in your life, they change little. They are formed during your childhood, but lived in your adulthood.

To identify your values in life, pretend that you are lying in your coffin and people are streaming past saying a variety of words about you. This is not intended to be morbid, but to help you understand what you want others to say about you during and after your life.

As the people pass by, quietly listen to the words. Let the words be specific. For example, they might be saying, "He was honest to a fault," or they might be saying, "He cheated me every time he could." "He was a great father," or, "I wish he had been around more when I was growing up," and so forth.

Listen to the words and you will see what runs your life. It may take a bit of introspection for the words to come out. Be honest with yourself. Don't try to sugar-coat it just to make yourself feel better. You are only cheating yourself.

List about five or six values. If you have more, prioritize the list and select the top five or six. Those are your driving values. Those are the values you want to strive to have. All your decisions and actions should be congruent to those values. It helps make life's decisions that much easier.

When I conduct a workshop where I have people go through this process, I time this part to be about fifteen minutes. Anything beyond that and too many ancillary values are written that are not germane to one's life. They are not really high-runners and therefore, will not really add to one's satisfaction.

Wright

Okay, once a person has the values listed, what is the next step?

Zimmer

The second step is to create your vision and mission statement.

The vision statement is your long-term view of what you want to become. This statement must be in line with your values from step one. My vision statement is: *I will live so that I am true to God, myself, and my fellowman. At the end of my days, while there may be some that say wrong things about me, I will know that I have dealt in honesty, integrity, love, and truthfulness to the fullest of my abilities.*

My top four values are:

- Integrity with God and myself
- Honesty in all affairs of life
- Love for my fellowman
- Truthful in all matters

While I am not perfect, those are my guiding factors.

The mission statement is how you will enact the vision statement. The mission statement provides the "how" to the vision statement.

My mission statement is: *I will live by the principles of God's Word. In all situations, I will be truthful and honest, even when it is not to my advantage. I will help those who want my help to the best of my abilities and seek to understand others before I try to be understood. I will be my greatest critic to make sure I follow my values.*

I am brutally honest with myself and my "performance." But by simply listing my values and creating my vision and mission statement for life, I have simplified many life decisions. I make those decisions in line with my core values, my vision, and my mission statements. Additionally, the simple fact that I spent time doing these two steps is well spent, educational time about David A. Zimmer—me!

Again, when I conduct a workshop, I usually time this part to be between fifteen to thirty minutes. Within that time period, the gist of the two statements can be constructed. Wordsmithing the statements can be done later if necessary.

Wright

I can see the step-wise refinement that you mentioned earlier. So after you have your vision statement—where you want to go—and your mission statement—the broad brush statement of how—what is the next step?

Zimmer

Step number three is to break your life into different areas and create specific goals that will help you reach your vision and mission statements. Again, the goals must align with the values, otherwise the contradiction will lead to very unsatisfying results.

I have broken life into six areas:

- Personal
- Spiritual
- Family
- Social
- Business/Professional
- Financial

The template has these six areas listed with one per page. This is the time-consuming part of the process. In my workshops, I usually let this step run between forty-five to sixty minutes.

I have the participants spread the six pages out in front of them so that each page is showing. I ask them to write down goals that come to mind and place them under the category where the goal most likely would fall.

For example, if one of my goals was to earn a college degree, I would place that under Personal. If a goal were to earn $100,000 per year, I would place that under Financial, and so on.

For me, the method of placing all the pages out in front of me works very well because I am a non-linear thinker. Ideas pop into my head almost in a random order, so I need to capture them on paper before they disappear.

Other people are more linear thinkers—they think about one topic at a time, complete that area, and move on to the next. That's fine with me. In that case, simply stack the papers up, focus on one area, and get the thoughts written.

Also, don't worry if a particular goal should appear under one category or another; that is not important. What is important is to capture the thought or goal onto paper—not the category that contains the goal.

A person finds that once he or she starts to write the goals down, then new goals start to come more rapidly. Capture them all. Once they are written, then go back and prioritize, move them around, erase them, etc.

This step simply lists the goals, but not the detailed steps to reach those goals. I save that for another time. At this point the participants are pretty tired from the introspection and thought process. Participants can prioritize, organize, and provide the detailed steps for goal completion at another time. They complete that portion at home and then send me the results by e-mail within two weeks. I know that those who complete this task and send me an e-mail within the time period are serious and will be successful.

Wright

That does sound like a lot of work. I guess anything worth having requires work.

Zimmer

That's right, David, success is a lot of work. There are many who want to reach success, but few who are willing to put in the effort to make it happen for them. Many start on the path and many give up. That is a shame.

The next step—Step Four—is to take stock of what you have and what you don't have to accomplish your goals. Now you must define your strengths and weaknesses. Your strengths will help you reach your goals and eventually your personal definition of success; but your weaknesses will hold you back, sometimes even stop you.

To overcome this issue, if you identify your weaknesses you can be creative in overcoming them. For example, let's say I want to be a professional speaker. My strengths might be my vast knowledge in a specific area, my super personality, my ability to network with people easily, and my knack of extracting the essence of a topic and putting it into understandable terms.

My weakness might be that I have a speech impediment that makes it difficult to fully understand what I am saying. For many, that impediment would stop them from reaching their goal. I need to determine how I might overcome that issue. One way is through voice training. I could hire a speech coach who can help me train my tongue to work in such a way as to make my speech more clear.

Another solution might be to examine which words give me particular difficulty and craft my message to not use those words. Or I might take extra time to practice those words so that I can say them clearly. A third way would be to team with another person who might act as my "interpreter" for the audience, and so on.

By listing my strengths and weaknesses, I can build upon my strengths and creatively overcome the weaknesses.

Wright

It looks like the plan is pretty complete. Are there any final steps?

Zimmer

There are three. The first is to finish the goal prioritization. Each goal should be broken down into workable, manageable steps so that you can accomplish something and see the progress being made.

The second is to track progress. That means you have to actively pursue the steps necessary to reach the goal, which may mean spending a specific amount of time daily, weekly, monthly, or whatever to make sure you are moving forward on the goal.

And the final step is to solicit help from others. No one has ever become successful in a vacuum. Those who are successful always had a group of supportive friends who would do whatever was necessary to help. Find a group of friends who will support you in your endeavors. That is the key to your success. And don't forget them once you have reached your success.

Always review your goals, revise them, and add new ones. Make sure they are in line with the values set forth at the beginning.

Wright

Thank you, David, for your insights. Our time is almost up. Do you have any closing thoughts?

Zimmer

Yes, I have two.

First, it says in the Bible in the book of Joshua, first chapter, to be "Strong and of good courage." In fact, God commands Joshua to be strong and of good courage three times. When someone tells me something three times, I usually sit up and take notice.

Becoming successful is a lot of work—often hard work. So don't give up. Be strong and of good courage. If you keep pressing on, you will find that the steps to each goal get accomplished and therefore, goals will be met. Meeting goals spurs you on to greater heights. Be strong and of good courage.

The second thought states "do not despise the day of small beginnings" (Zechariah 4:10). This means that a small success is better than no success. Many times the small beginning is not the big bang that we want, so we toss out the small successes as nothing. By doing so, we rob ourselves of the next win, the next success and therefore, we slowly erode away our ability to achieve our goals. Count each success as something precious and build on it to meet your goals. Success is a journey to becoming who you want to become. It starts out one step at a time. Every long journey starts out with a single step—sometimes a small step.

Take the step. Enjoy the small beginnings. And make them mount up until you have reached your success.

About the Author

DAVID A. ZIMMER is an author, speaker, and recognized authority in project management. He conducts seminars and workshops for small and large companies in the area of project management. While many think of project management as purely managing schedules and budgets, project managers must have many more skills.

To be an effective project manager, Mr. Zimmer learned that he must be a student of life and people. His personal research and study in understanding people, their interaction, and requirements for success spans several decades. He developed the Tactical Plan for Success to help others who came to him for guidance and understanding in turning their lives around.

Being successful in any endeavor requires following a plan to achieve goals. The largest step for people in this process is to understand themselves. Mr. Zimmer's time- and people-tested method helps many reach their level of success personally, professionally, and financially.

Mr. Zimmer's Tactical Plan for Success breaks life into six areas and helps a person navigate his or her success journey. By following the Tactical plan, you can be the next success story.

David A. Zimmer
American Eagle Group
P.O. Box 703
Warrington, PA 18976
Phone: 215.491.2544
Fax: 215.491.2545
E-mail: info@ameagle.com
www.ameagle.com

Chapter 9

BARB SCHWARZ, ASPM, IAHSP, AB, RLS, CSP

THE INTERVIEW

David Wright (Wright)

Today we're talking with Barb Schwarz. She is a leader, an innovator, and a truly gifted speaker who shares the wisdom of her personal triumphs. Those who experience Barb are always struck by her incredible energy as well as the valuable substance of her programs. Internationally known as the creator of Home Staging and Founder of StagedHomes.com and the International Association of Home Staging Professionals, Barb is a savvy businesswoman and CEO, best-selling author, and radio and television personality.

Barb's new book, *Home Staging: The Winning Way to Sell Your House for More Money,* has received rave reviews nationally. Barb has recently been featured on ABC's *20/20,* NBC's *The Today Show,* Fox News, and CBS's *Evening News.*

Barb Schwarz invented the concept of Staging a home and she has literally built the Home Staging industry. She has developed the Accredited Staging Professional (ASP) course to set, maintain, and guide the principles and practices of the Home Staging industry she created. She has traveled extensively, beginning in 1985 to the present, teaching over one million Real Estate Agents and Professional Home Stagers throughout North America.

Barb, welcome to *Speaking of Success.*

Barb Schwarz (Schwarz)

It's wonderful to be with you.

Wright

What personal experiences do you touch upon for motivation?

Schwarz

I think it always comes back to intent. As anyone sets about doing a job, a career, or a mission—and looking back on my life, I really am on a mission—it goes back to the "intent" of what the purpose in the person's mission is about. As we delve into what the intent is, it is very self-motivating. When you work for the highest good of all concerned, and when it's to the harm of no one, there is absolutely nothing on the planet that will keep what you want from happening. When you have the highest good of all concerned in your heart, mind, and soul you will achieve your intent. That to me is self-motivating and that is what I get back to all the time—my intent—and what my mission is, and how I work to achieve that each and every day.

Wright

What is your definition of success?

Schwarz

One of my mentors is Albert Einstein, even though I've never known him. I would love to have been able to sit at his feet. He has a wonderful saying that I quote in my seminars and training sessions: *"Let us not strive to be people of success, but rather people of value."* When we are of value to our clients and our communities, our families, and our companies, then and only then are we truly successful. I'm always talking about value—what value-added services do we offer to our clientele, our students, audiences, neighbors, friends, and family? It's all about value.

Wright

What is the foundation of your success?

Schwarz

I've been looking back and thinking about my life. I've had some life adventures in the past six to seven years that I've chosen to learn from. I see them as gifts rather than negative experiences. I've looked back and asked, "What is my foundation?" I think the answer is faith and believing in the gifts I've been given.

Believe in yourself; believe in your purpose and in your mission. People say, "Well, I'll believe it when I see it." But I say, "You will see it when you believe it! I believe that our affirmations and how we talk to ourselves is far more important than what we hear from others. How we talk to others is a reflection of how we talk and think about ourselves. Affirmations work on improving my communication with myself and are a very strong foundation.

Believing in a higher power is another foundation that I think is important. No matter what you call that higher power, I think it's very crucial that we believe in something greater than ourselves individually. It's important to believe that we are a part of that higher power as a part of us. So, in my opinion, when you have that as your foundation and you use it with the intent to keep you strong with your mission and purpose, you have a solid foundation. The Bible says that a building without a firm foundation will crumble and fall.

I find that setting those guidelines and principles for myself keeps me focused and helps me have that mission-driven life each and every day.

Wright

What is the major milestone in your career?

Schwarz

I haven't often stopped to look back until recently, even though I've mentioned it a couple of times here. I think it's easier to see the past as we look back, if we choose to do that from time to time as we get a bit older.

When I look at my twenties and thirties it was, "What is this all about?" In my forties it started to gel more, and then in my fifties, I can see that the reason I taught school was because it was getting me ready to teach all the people who have come to my training sessions. I believe sales is all about education—you educate your client and your customers. You are paid according to your ability to educate because you don't "sell" anybody anything.

Then I look back at my design career. I have three degrees from the University of Washington—one in education, one in music, and one in design. After college graduation I thought I was going to be Barbra Streisand, but I ended up Barb Schwarz—I get to say my message instead of sing it.

As I set up my design business years ago I learned a lot in that business, which I had for five years. I made a lot of mistakes that later really paid off in a positive way when I then got into Real Estate.

As I got into Real Estate and began to teach my sellers about what to do and what not to do, that's when I invented the Home Staging Concept. That was clear back in 1972. Little did I know that I would become one of the top producers of Real Estate in Seattle. That led to others wanting to know about my invention of Home Staging, which then birthed my speaking career.

So my teaching ability moved me into my design business, the design business helped move me into the Real Estate industry, and I began to see the antithesis of that. I began to see how decorating just didn't make any sense in Real Estate because I wanted to depersonalize the house where decorating the house is personalizing it. Then the idea of Staging came to me. When we Stage a house we depersonalize it so that it will be more attractive to potential buyers. Buyers can more easily picture themselves in a house that has minimal decorating features. They can more easily see a house's potential.

Then in 1985 all of those skills came together in the birth of my speaking career. From 1985 to 1998 I spoke to over 1,000,000 people from the platform.

As a speaker in 1998, one of the main messages I wanted to share with people was to listen to their intuition. I think it's a sixth sense. I also believe it's a gift from God. I think it's our "inner knower" and when I don't listen to it I run into cement walls, figuratively speaking. As I do listen to it, even though I may not understand it, it has always proved to be of value to others and myself.

In 1998 I had this feeling—this nudge on the inside—that I should leave the platform. A lot of my speaker friends thought I was a little bit crazy to give up my professional speaking career, but I said, "I'm not giving it up—I'm just putting it aside." I went back into the Real Estate industry as a Real Estate agent in 1998 and I moved to a very special spot called Whidbey Island. No one knew me there—no one had heard of me there—and I started selling real estate again.

Now, looking back, I realize that if I hadn't listened to my inner voice I never would have come up with the accreditation of ASP for Home Staging Professionals and for Realtors and for the Staging industry. I developed, invented, and am building the Home Staging Industry and the ASP Designations to this very day. It was during that time that I determined I was going to create a more involved, detailed training called the ASP Training Course for the Accredited Staging Professional for the Real Estate industry and for the home Staging industry. And that is exactly what I did.

At that time I also felt a "nudge" to develop and found the International Association of Home Staging Professionals mentioned in my introduction.

A day later during this certain time, I came up with the idea of The Staging University; it is the only one in the world. It is online for all of our graduates around the world because we are worldwide right now.

All of these things happened because I went back into the Real Estate industry and continued working in the industry for five years. I truly believe if I had not listened to that inner voice this might not have happened. There would not be a Stagedhomes.com, an ASP Designation, a Staging University, nor would the International Association of Home Staging Professionals have been created. Going back into Real Estate and listening to that inner knower—that inner voice—is what that inner voice was all about. My spirit knew it at the time but my head did not.

Now I look at all that has come from it and I encourage people to listen to that voice inside.

As all of this began to develop more and more, I decided to return to the training and speaking platform. Each piece has been so important in my own world to help other people and to serve them.

I happen to believe that all people can look back and see pieces of their lives like a quilt leading them to their greatest work ahead. My greatest work is yet to come. I believe that those who read this book and who read this message need to know that they haven't yet achieved their greatest work yet either. That's why we are still on this great planet earth—to continue to grow in serving each other—and our greatest service is yet to come in the work that lies ahead for us all.

Wright

What do you think holds people back from obtaining their goals more than anything else?

Schwarz

One main word: *fear.* Fear can be defined in many ways. I like the definition: "False evidence appearing real." Fear comes from our brain and our ego.

I believe that living in spirit and in the creativity we've been given and listening to that inner knower is where the heart is located. The phrase "follow your heart; it will never let you down" is so true. The heart is where your spirit and love lives.

People are either moving from love or moving from fear. Fear is what holds everyone back, and fears are false illusions. People say, "Oh, I won't make enough money," or, "Oh gosh, what if my spouse divorces me?" or, "Gee, what if the interest rates change or what if the economy goes bad? Oh my gosh, what's going to happen?" I'll tell you what, you've never not made money, all of you who are listening or reading—everything always works out! Have you ever had a challenge that you've never been able to solve in one way or another? Somehow you've always solved everything that has ever confronted you. Therefore I like to call problems "opportunities."

Years ago we used the term "problems," then a lot of people started calling them "challenges." In the place where I am coming from now I consider them opportunities because having that mindset is where we learn.

It is fear that holds us back. We must walk through fear and/or set fear aside. The best thing is to confront fears and move on! Someone said to me a long time ago, "Your mind is like a parachute—if it's not open it doesn't work!" Everybody reading this book is an intelligent human being, yet you may hear a warning that, "Someone might put some junk in your mind." You are adult enough and intelligent and creative enough to know when something sounds like junk or not. So keep an open mind and an open heart, and listen to your heart more than your mind.

One of the things that I believe and say is, "Stop your thinking and change your life." We analyze everything to pieces; we analyze, analyze, analyze!

The ego is what keeps us back and that is where fear is based. So when you confront your fears and move through them, doors open up and the very thing that you want is out there just waiting for you.

Wright
When is your creative time of day?

Schwarz
My creative time of day is when I get into my faith zone—when I listen to that voice inside. It can be any time of the day. Deepak Copra calls it "the zone." I love what he and others have to say. I have been a follower of Deepak Chopra's work and of the work of others in this book for many, many years. The "gap" or "the zone" (as many athletes call it), or that "space," is sometimes when you go to bed before you fall asleep. It might be just as you wake up in the morning. You may be one of those who don't jump right out of bed, but instead you let your intuition or inner knower process come through.

For me it can be when I'm driving the car. Sometimes it's when I'm sitting and waiting for an appointment, or during an appointment with someone else. It's when I say to myself, "Get quiet, go inside, and allow the voice to come through."

It's not that I hear outer voices—it's that I know when I know that I know! It's when you get that nudge, that gentle feeling that gets stronger and stronger; I call it the creative genius within. Most people have never written that down. So why not write down: "I am a creative genius!" I ask everyone in my trainings to do that! Our teachers should have our children do that in school. For far too long we have listened to the judgments of others and we still do it today. We listen to others more than we should as they say to us, "Oh, that's a stupid idea, you'll never make any money with that." People may mean well, including our neighbors and friends, etc., but you have to remember that they have fears too and often they are forecasting fear from themselves onto you.

Getting into your zone is getting into that place where you feel you are tapped into the creative. It could be at the strangest times—it could be in an elevator or whenever. I used to have to wait for it to come to me but these days I'm finding it easier and easier to tap into it at any time. The more you ask, the more you listen, and the more you listen, the easier it is—at least that has been my experience. The knowledge is there. Knowledge is energy. Energy is knowledge.

I'm a big follower of quantum physics. I loved the movie *What the Bleep Do We Know?* It has had a definite impact on many people. Even if you don't like part of it, don't tune out the whole movie. It is a controversial 2004 film that combines documentary interviews and a fictional narrative to posit a connection between science and spirituality. It features various interviews with individuals presented as experts in science and spirituality who discuss quantum physics and how we can change our minds and open up the flow.

I've learned that it's all about the energy, and the energy is there for everyone to tap into! So to me, those nudges and those feelings inside are a gift from God—a beautiful energy that we have the ability to tap into as long as we are working for good. As we work for good we are able to manifest good things and we are able to mold and shape them. I believe that when we desire the highest good for all concerned, nothing can keep it from happening. As we use the energy for good, it brings so much more prosperity to all of us; it has a ripple effect and positively affects everyone.

I think there is much more "good" energy on the planet and there are good people and good spirits. Good intent on the planet far outweighs what we would perceive as "not good;" so it's all about tapping into that. Think it, believe in the good energy, look for it, support it, affirm it, and create more of it.

Wright

So how do you manifest good things into your life?

Schwarz

I love that question, thank you for asking. I used to say, "Oh I wish I could have that. Oh I really wish . . . " There's a song that starts, "A dream is a wish . . ." (from the Disney animated movie *Cinderella*). In a way it's almost like we think it can't happen. As you get into that zone, whatever that means to you (you could call it prayer or meditation), you're not wishing for it but rather, you are believing in it very calmly. You're not begging for it, you're stating it in the present as if it's already happened.

The principles that I've carved out for my own life begin this way:

1. Believe in a higher power.
2. Believe that you are a part of that power and that that power is a part of you.
3. Believe that what you want already exists because it does! What doesn't exist that you want? It's already there, and if you don't see it physically it's in the energy field that I've just talked about.
4. Be thankful for it before it ever shows up.

In a big way Home Staging is really about love. When we help people sell their properties faster and for more money people say thank you and tell us that they love what we did for them!

We see children who are on Ritalin or other prescriptions and their rooms are just a disaster and a cluttered mess. Then, after we de-clutter the room, parents will tell us that their child sleeps better. That is about love too. We have made it a peaceful, joyful, and very simple environment. In Home Staging, "less is more." All of a sudden the parent says, "You've just changed my child's life and our life and we love you for that." Well, that is a big deal; and it's about love.

Then there is the ninety-five-year-old who couldn't sell his house. His wife had died from cancer a year or two before. We Staged his house and it sold for top dollar. Well, that is about love too! We were able to Stage his house and have it sell using the very things he al-ready had that were very old and some not very attractive. We crea-tively set the Stage with those items and his property sold for $45,000 more, even in a tough market. Well, that is about helping people and bringing love to the man and his property too. Why? Because it al-lowed him to then have more time in a beautiful retirement home or adult family home instead of going to a county facility that would not have been as nice. He looked at me with tears in his eyes and said, "Barb, I really love you for this."

That's what my business is really all about. That's where the in-tent, that's where the purpose, that's where moving the energy all comes together to create more good for all. Staging is about energy— it's about changing the energy in the property. As we do what we do we bring that value out of service, spreading love, and we see creativ-ity right in front of us. It's believing and manifesting the good by moving the energy and seeing it in the way we believed in, even be-fore it happened in reality.

This is what I want to create in our world. This is what I want my business to be about—creating good things for good people through the use of good energy working for the good of all concerned. By doing that and sharing it with others I am hopefully living the affirmation.

My friends say, "You're possessed," and I say, "Yes I am!" You could say I'm possessed by this mission I'm on. There are plenty of things that could get in the way, but I won't allow it. I'm moving through obstacles by positive affirmations, by believing, and being thankful for more good things before they ever show up.

The fifth principle I follow is, "Let go and let God." As we do that, we allow what we want to create and have happen to manifest in the best positive way for all concerned. Sometimes we have blinders on and we don't see the good. We expect it to come from straight ahead but it comes from left field or right field. We have to be open to where the good can come from. When we do that we are going to have more good than we ever imagined.

There is a phrase that goes, "If you knew who walked beside you, you would not be afraid." I believe in that too. I also believe that if you knew all the good that God had in mind for you on this earth and in this Universe, you would not let anything stop you. There are people who want to support you, to help you be successful and have value. When you begin to come from that place, then you will see all the great things that are out there!

I am told that many, many years ago a saint said that it is not our darkness that scares us; what really scares us is our light—we are afraid of what we really can create. (Mary Anne Williamson and Nelson Mandela have both used that quote also.)

So believe in a higher power; know that it's on the inside of you. Believe and know that everything you ever wanted is out there waiting for you. Be thankful for it before it ever shows up, and then let go and let God, and just get on with taking the steps of action and trust that the good is on its way to you.

Wright

How do you learn to take risks?

Schwarz

By taking them! To quote Guillaume Apollinaire: "Come to the edge, he said. They said: We are afraid. Come to the edge, he said. They came. He pushed them and they flew."

We have eagles on Whidbey Island where one of my offices is. I'm told the mother eagle builds her nest with feathers and soft items she finds. But at the very bottom of the nest she builds it with thorns. As the babies grow, the down feathers begin to collapse and soon the babies feel the thorns that eventually urge them to fly.

So do what you want to do—you need to fly too. Take the fear and move through it when you are ready. You can do it one step at a time. When you really, really believe, there is only one thing that works and that is to take action.

I grew up on a farm in Kansas. My Grandpa Sam is one of my heroes. He's long since left the planet, however, I still hear his words. He used to say to me in the orchard, "Barbie, if you want the fruit, you've got to crawl out on a limb to get it." I've never forgotten that. In fact, recently in one of the department stores, I saw that there were red slippers with those actual words written on the toes. (Of course I had to buy them!) What I dare myself to do is confront the fear and move through it.

People can get depressed and people can stop and people can get discouraged, but the key is to face it and take action.

I was just answering an e-mail from one of my students who graduated from my ASP course. She was confronting some fears too. I wrote to her to take action. Action is the best healer for all of us. Just a simple step of taking an action, and then another step; step by step you are on your way. We all know the Chinese saying that a journey of thousand miles begins with one single step—so don't allow yourself to be immobilized by fear. Take a step, take action, and that will lead you to the next step as well.

Wright

When did you know your calling?

Schwarz

I was five years old, and that's the truth. Some people say that when they were young they knew, and I am one of them. I actually felt that when I was five years old I would do something significant in my life. I did not know what it would be, but I remember actually feeling that something I would do would help make a difference. That has propelled me even to this very day.

That feeling, that nudge, that inner voice has gotten stronger and stronger through the years. Sometimes I wandered off the path and sometimes I felt that what I was doing was not leading me to where I was supposed to be. The key though has been to always get back to my faith and take action based upon it.

Growing up I had a feeling in the pit of my stomach that really used to bother me. It was a feeling that there was more—there had to be more. What I've learned is that I would get that feeling when I wasn't being all that I could be. Today I do not experience that feeling in the pit of my stomach as often as I used to. When and if I get off track it still comes back though. So I move forward and now most of the time I don't have that feeling as much anymore.

It was a pushing feeling that was nudging me on the inside. I didn't always know where it came from or what it was about. That is where listening to intuition is so crucial. The key again is to get out of fear and to take steps of action. Now I look back and realize that this is the mission I was given. I know it now more than ever because of the experiences I've shared with you and the careers I've had. This is what it's about—to bring service to others and to share generosity and love and good spirit. In my case it's through training and teaching the magic of Home Staging.

Wright

I'm told you are very in tune with your "inner voice." When faced with two choices, one being a logical path to success and the other something your heart is telling you to do, which do choose and why?

Schwarz

I choose the heart. I learned many years ago from my inner voice that I know that I know that I know, and I encourage others to listen to their own inner voice.

In the year 2002 I felt a nudge to move from Whidbey Island to California. My husband did not want to go. "Are you nuts?" he said. "What are you doing? We're so happy here." I said that I had to go— God told Noah to build an ark and he did it. If God told me to "build an ark," I would build an ark! That's how strong the feeling was.

I felt that voice when I got into Real Estate, and that was in 1972. I knew that it was something I was being called to do.

In 1985 I'd listened to that voice urging me to become a professional speaker. I'd had no training but it just seemed to be a gift that was given to me when I got on the platform. Now I have perfected it through the years in all the ways that I could.

In 1998 I'd listened to that voice; it took us to Whidbey Island from Bellevue, Washington.

Then, a year ago November, I felt I was to go to Chicago. And now I have an office in Chicago. So when people say to me, "Where do you live?" I always tell them that I live on the planet! I mean it. I go where I am directed to go—to live where I am directed to live. I've learned to just go with that flow, not to fight it, and listen to that inner knower. Stay in tune and balance it. I call it "Spiritual Intelligence." Those are my words for it. Spiritual intelligence brings the two together—the spirit and intelligence. I am not suggesting that you stick your head in the sand. I think of the spirit as being on the inside. I gather all the facts and get all the information about whatever the goal is. Then I apply spiritual intelligence and the answers come—they always come forth.

Being in tune with one's inner voice is about the feeling that you have inside, and when you hear that little nudge to "live here" or "don't do that" or "don't push it" or "hire this person" or "don't hire this person," follow it! Follow what I call your spiritual intelligence—it will never let you down.

Wright

Who has inspired you?

Schwarz

I mentioned Einstein; I'm very inspired by him. I'm also very much a follower of Leonardo da Vinci's work. I have a screen-saver that has his artwork on it, and I have books that have been written about him. I also have a lot of books with his art printed inside. My Grandpa Sam and his gentle spirit has also inspired me.

We never know who "the disciples" or "the Christs" among us might be. Regardless of what your faith or mine is, I use that term in the highest sense. Those who inspire us are the ones who love without fear, who give without fear, and who extend helping hands to others. They could be the Buddhists among us too. There are many good, kind spirits among us. It could be the person in the tollbooth—it's not so much their profession, it's how they lead their day-to-day lives. We come into this life without anything and we will leave with nothing. It's the journey, not the destination.

I also have great respect for Eleanor Roosevelt; I have read a lot about her. I've also followed Frank Lloyd Wright's work.

As I see our leaders today I'm constantly looking for those who get out of self and get out of ego to share better ideas with others. I look for leaders who come from the standpoint of service.

Wright

What are some of the toughest lessons you've learned?

Schwarz

I've followed my intuition for so many years now; I think the toughest lesson has been to love myself. We are taught to love others. I was raised in a very strict way in the "Bible Belt" in Kansas. There are many good things that came from that, but at the same time my creativity was sometimes discouraged. It was encouraged, however, by my grandpa. It seems that it took all the way into my 50s for me to really accept who I was. I was always afraid that people might not like what I was saying or thinking or who I really was.

In the year 2000 I became very sick. My illness made a huge impact on my life. I developed an infection that spread to my heart from my stomach and I ended up having heart surgery. I almost didn't make it. In fact, I died twice and had an afterlife experience to a point. I left the planet and I was sent back both times (that is another book in and of itself). This year, for my third heart surgery they told me, "We're going to keep you awake this time because you left us the last two times!"

I lost my father this year to that evil disease, Alzheimer's. Those of us who have lost loved ones don't need to be concerned about them. We miss them and we have sorrow because we miss them, but I was "on the other side" long enough to know that death is nothing to fear—it's actually the next journey, the next chapter. The spirit is eternal. I often call people angels because I saw angels. Someone can poke holes in that all they want, however, it has happened to me twice and it was very, very powerful.

I believe I was sent back to spread the concept of Staging around the world because it is a way of training one person at a time, Staging one home at a time, and changing lives one family at a time. It spreads the message of service, value, and love. Staging is not about things, it is about people. When we Stage a house, we reduce the number of items in every room. We have so much stuff in our houses that we can't appreciate each other as much anymore. Where you live should reflect you—you should be the star. It should be about your family and celebrating that—not all the things and the clutter we have around us. I sometimes find that people with the most clutter have the most issues; not always, but sometimes I find that to be true. By Staging we see a lot of their issues simply dissipate.

I think my biggest lesson has been to finally accept who I am and to really begin to love myself. We all make mistakes and we all have issues within us. We don't seem to have the same love for ourselves that we show for others. This is true of women especially—as women we multi-task so much. As women we end up serving others—our children, our spouses, community projects, employers—so much that the last person we take care of is ourselves. So that's something I've really needed to learn.

One of my friends observed, "It is interesting that the infection affected your heart, Barb, because you have such a big heart." My illness taught me a lesson too. I learned that I have to have a heart for myself as well as for others.

I have a saying on my wall, a quote from Rabbi Hillel, that reads, *"If I am not for myself, then who will be? And if I am only for myself then who am I?"* That is very powerful and says it best.

I believe that you can't sell anything unless you yourself are sold on it. Believing in yourself—in what you do and who you are, and the values and the mission and the purpose that you have—will then empower others to join you. So it comes back to not coming from the ego, it's about coming from the heart.

I am glad to be alive here and now. I am glad to see my invention of Home Staging begin to come into its own here and all around the world too. I am very much a person of the heart.

Cardiologists have actually found that the heart does have feelings! Leading cardiologists have told me that they can now actually document this. The heart is where it begins and where it ends. There really is no ending though as we make the transition—we just go to the next beginning.

Wright

How do you deal with fears and apprehensions?

Schwarz

The only way is to take the action that I mentioned. The analyzing is where we get stuck. One can always find reasons not to do something. The "not" is where the fear lives, and the "do" is where it's out of the box. During my presentations I'll draw a box up on the screen. We all carry this box around with us; it's called "the fear box" and it lives on the inside of everyone.

I was taught a long time ago by a psychologist to pretend and use the Jack-in-the-Box toy I used to have as a kid. She said that when I have challenges, to mentally place them in my pretend Jack-in-the-Box. Visualize shutting the lid and then don't worry about them anymore.

When we say the words "worry" or "fear" or "objection," it changes the chemistry of the brain. When you say the word "concern" instead of "fear," or "concern" instead of "worry," or "concern" instead of "objection," it feels so much better! So I don't choose the word "fear." Instead, I say that I have a concern. I don't use the words "objection" or "worry." Words matter and those are just a few that I use and a few I avoid. The words you use have a real effect upon you and others too.

I also ask myself, "How do I feel about this? What is my inner knower saying?" I get to that still, small place inside and the answer comes. It used to take about three years to manifest things I wanted to see, but now I'm able to say it sometimes takes just three seconds! Sometimes it's three days. Sometimes it's almost instantly. My colleagues and friends say, "Welcome to Barb's world—things happen very fast here!" They really do, and it's all about believing and getting into that inner-knower—the genius within and the creativity within—and living there as best you can. The only way to do it is to take a step and begin.

Wright

What three strengths are the most important to build on to become successful?

Schwarz

First of all is "intent"—what is your intent; what is your purpose? Those are very important strengths.

I think that being very persistent and not giving up is very important. I have a Winston Churchill quote on the inside of my front door that says, *"Never, never, never give up!"* When you believe in something, your persistence is crucial.

Then coming from a place of value is very important. What are we doing that is of value to others? What services can we provide? It's not just about the money. Yes, we all want money to have a wonderful way of life, and money allows us to do things for others; but it doesn't have to cost a dime to give something to others. You can give them an idea or a pat on the back. You can volunteer your time and be helpful wherever you feel needed.

The words that come to me the most vividly are: "intent," "persistence," and "value."

Truth is also a very, very important word. What is your truth, how do you feel it? How do you know it? And are you a person of integrity? Your word should be your word; the only one you cheat is you. The only one you really let down is you. When you stand for who you are, and you gather all the strength you have on the inside, go ahead and express how you feel and do it in a caring way. Communication is another very important key as part of the foundation of everything that you do.

I'm still learning every day; I'm not there yet, and the evidence for this is that I'm still on the planet. I was at one of the department stores awhile ago. I needed a particular kind of towel and I couldn't find them. I asked a store clerk if she could find them, and off she went to see if she could. By the look on her face I could tell that she wasn't having the best day. As she left I turned around and all of a sudden I found the towels. When I looked up she was coming toward me carrying the towels. She said, "Oh I found the towels!" Now, what I share with you next is just a wee example of what I strive to do each day. I could have turned to her and just said, "Oh, don't bother, I already found them," but what good would that have done for her spirit? How would that have made her feel honored? I turned to her and I just said, "I am so grateful to you for finding them. Thank you so much for doing that." She handed them to me and went on her merry way. From the smile on her face I could tell that finding the towels for me had helped make her day. Previously, she had looked discouraged and she'd had a frown on her face. Now, all of sudden, there was a swing in her step and she had a big smile on her face! Rather than my saying, "I don't need them anymore, I already found them," which would have totally demoralized her, I thanked her.

If I had said I had found them and didn't need them she might have thought, "What am I even here for when I'm not able to help?" So whether I needed all the towels or not doesn't matter. I restocked the shelf with a couple of them and then I bought two of the ones she brought to me.

One of the words that mean so much to me is "honoring." I wrote a code of ethics for our ASP Accredited Professional Real Estate Agents and our Accredited Staging Professional Stagers. Because I invented this industry of Home Staging I have set guidelines and ethical standards for it. I have felt that it was my mission to set the policies and practices to guide the industry. In that code of ethics, honoring the client is number one on the list.

When someone walks up to me during one of my training sessions, my goal is to always be the same off the platform as I am on the platform. All of us are speakers and teachers whether we have a large audience or an audience of one such as our neighbor or friend or relative, and we should honor those we speak to just as we honor ourselves.

Sometimes someone will come up to me and say excitedly, "Oh my gosh, I've got this great idea, this is what you ought to do." Well, the truth is (and this happens to me quite a bit) that I've usually already thought of it. But rather than saying something that would totally demoralize the person, what I want to do in my communication is honor him or her. It' another way to help make someone's day special by saying, "That is such a great idea, thank you so much for sharing that with me." I haven't told an untruth—it's the absolute truth that I'm very grateful for the suggestion because it is supportive and indicates that I must be on the right track. I also want to acknowledge others for being open to share their ideas, and not discourage them by saying that it's a silly idea. (So many of us have been told that all of our lives.) I could also say, "I was thinking about something like that and you have just helped me feel that I'm on the right track. You are great, thank you so much!"

I do that every single day. When my feet hit the floor in the morning it's my goal to help empower others as well as myself, and to honor others so that everyone I come in contact with can have a better day. By doing that I have a better day too because we are mirroring each other. You see, we only know what we are. When people come up and say, "Barb, you're just the greatest" (and I'm very blessed that someone would do that) or, "You've changed my life," what I say to that person is, "I really didn't change your life—I shared a message with you and you were willing to take the action. Isn't it great that we are getting to know each other? Hopefully we can help serve each other and be of value together more."

No matter how much I have become known through Home Staging, it's very important to me to stay humble and grounded. Sure, I have an ego—everybody has an ego—the key is to honor others and mirror back what we want to experience ourselves.

Wright

As a woman in business who inspires other women, how do you feel about women helping other women versus being competitive?

Schwarz

I believe that women love to help other women! My goal is to work together with them and to honor them. In so doing I reach others and the circle of giving continues on.

I'm so blessed to be a member of the National Speakers Association and I see it there as well. I love the NSA and I've tried very hard to carry the same integrity into the International Association of Home Staging Professionals, which I founded in 2000. The majority of the 12,000 people I've trained since then have been women and these women love to work with and support other women. I've also been blessed to teach over a million Real Estate agents, and the majority of them have been women also. They love to serve the community of women and men.

Many of our 12,000 ASPs have formed into over one hundred chapters. I see them teaming up and helping each other with their businesses. They share ideas and techniques in the Home Staging field. What a joy and what a blessing that is! Women helping and supporting other women! And now, through our IAHSP Association, we have the Staging Service Week to help Stage homes for women and children and men in need throughout the communities in which we live and work. I am seeing a dream of mine coming true through the IAHSP Foundation and Charitable Staging Service Day I founded as women reach out to other women and men each year in this way too!

Wright

In your opinion, what is the biggest misconception people have about success?

Schwarz

That success means you become rich in dollars, which people call wealth. That kind of success can be fleeting. That success can go to people's heads. Using wealth as a standard is a misconception. First of all, success is not necessarily equated to how much money one makes. There are many people who are very successful but don't make a lot of money. I go back to Albert Einstein's real definition, *"Let us not strive to be people of success, but be people of value."* I would like to see people value others who do not earn millions of dollars but who are nonetheless successful because they are of value to the communities they serve.

Success doesn't have to be fleeting. Success is a state of mind. Being valuable is being of service to others. You are successful when you are of value to others.

I believe that the true leaders of today in companies and community service groups are people who don't have big egos. Our ASP Stagers and Real Estate agents are people who don't have big egos. They are coming from that place of serving people in their cities, states, and in countries around the world.

To me, people of success are people of value and they make a difference in the lives of all those around them.

Wright

Well, what a great conversation. I really appreciate your investing all this time with me today answering all these questions. You have given me a lot to think about, and I'm sure that you have also given our readers a lot to think about!

Schwarz

It's been my pleasure. It's been a true honor working with you. I send the best to all the people at your great company and all those you serve. I admire the way you are honoring so many people by spreading their mission, their words, and their values. So thank you! It's been a total joy, and I look forward to working with you again!

Wright

Today we have been talking with Barb Schwarz. Barb is a leader, an innovator, and a gifted speaker as we have found here today. Having taught over a million people, she believes in sharing her wisdom. She is internationally known as the creator of Home Staging. She is the founder of StageHome.com and the International Association of Home Staging Professionals. She is a great businesswoman, a best-selling author, and a radio and television personality.

Barb, thank you so much for being with us today on *Speaking of Success.*

Schwarz

You are so welcome. The pleasure was all mine.

About the Author

BARB SCHWARZ is a leader, an innovator, and a truly gifted speaker who shares the wisdom of her personal triumphs. Those who experience Barb are always struck by her incredible energy as well as the valuable substance of her programs. Internationally known as the creator of Home Staging and Founder of StagedHomes.com and the International Association of Home Staging Professionals, Barb is a savvy businesswoman and CEO, best-selling author, and radio and television personality.

Barb's new book, *Home Staging: The Winning Way to Sell Your House for More Money,* has received rave reviews nationally. Barb has recently been featured on ABC's *20/20,* NBC's *The Today Show,* Fox News, and CBS's *Evening News.*

Barb Schwarz invented the concept of Staging a home and she has literally built the Home Staging industry. She has developed the Accredited Staging Professional (ASP) course to set, maintain, and guide the principles and practices of the Home Staging industry she created. She has traveled extensively beginning in 1985 to the present, teaching over one million Real Estate Agents and Professional Home Stagers throughout North America.

Barb Schwarz, ASPM, IAHSP, AB, RLS
Certified Speaking Professional, CSP
Stagedhomes.com
2807 Clayton Rd, Suite 200
Concord, CA 94520
Phone: 800.392.7161
E-mail: barb@stagedhomes.com
www.stagedhomes.com

Chapter 10

JACK CANFIELD

David E. Wright (Wright)

Today we are talking with Jack Canfield. You probably know him as the founder and co-creator of the *New York Times* number one best-selling *Chicken Soup for the Soul* book series. As of 2006 there are sixty-five titles and eighty million copies in print in over thirty-seven languages.

Jack's background includes a BA from Harvard, a master's from the University of Massachusetts, and an Honorary Doctorate from the University of Santa Monica. He has been a high school and university teacher, a workshop facilitator, a psychotherapist, and a leading authority in the area of self-esteem and personal development.

Jack Canfield, welcome to *Speaking of Success.*

Jack Canfield (Canfield)

Thank you, David. It's great to be with you.

Wright

I talked with Mark Victor Hansen a few days ago. He gave you full credit for coming up with the idea of the *Chicken Soup* series. Obviously it's made you an internationally known personality. Other than recognition, has the series changed you personally and if so, how?

Canfield

I would say that it has and I think in a couple of ways. Number one, I read stories all day long of people who've overcome what would feel like insurmountable obstacles. For example, we just did a book *Chicken Soup for the Unsinkable Soul.* There's a story in there about a single mother with three daughters. She contracted a disease and she had to have both of her hands and both of her feet amputated. She got prosthetic devices and was able to learn how to use them. She could cook, drive the car, brush her daughters' hair, get a job, etc. I read that and I thought, "God, what would I ever have to complain and whine and moan about?"

At one level it's just given me a great sense of gratitude and appreciation for everything I have and it has made me less irritable about the little things.

I think the other thing that's happened for me personally is my sphere of influence has changed. By that I mean I was asked, for example, a couple of years ago to be the keynote speaker to the Women's Congressional Caucus. The Caucus is a group that includes all women in America who are members of Congress and who are state senators, governors, and lieutenant governors. I asked what they wanted me to talk about—what topic.

"Whatever you think we need to know to be better legislators," was the reply.

I thought, "Wow, they want me to tell them about what laws they should be making and what would make a better culture." Well, that wouldn't have happened if our books hadn't come out and I hadn't become famous. I think I get to play with people at a higher level and have more influence in the world. That's important to me because my life purpose is inspiring and empowering people to live their highest vision so the world works for everybody. I get to do that on a much bigger level than when I was just a high school teacher back in Chicago.

Wright

I think one of the powerful components of that book series is that you can read a positive story in just a few minutes and come back and revisit it. I know my daughter has three of the books and she just reads them interchangeably. Sometimes I go in her bedroom and she'll be crying and reading one of them. Other times she'll be laughing, so they really are "chicken soup for the soul," aren't they?

Canfield

They really are. In fact we have four books in the *Teenage Soul* series now and a new one coming out at the end of this year. I have a son who's eleven and he has a twelve-year-old friend who's a girl. We have a new book called *Chicken Soup for the Teenage Soul and the Tough Stuff.* It's all about dealing with parents' divorces, teachers who don't understand you, boyfriends who drink and drive, and other issues pertinent to that age group. I asked my son's friend, "Why do you like this book?" (It's our most popular book among teens right now.) She said, "You know, whenever I'm feeling down I read it and it makes me cry and I feel better. Some of the stories make me laugh and some of the stories make me feel more responsible for my life. But basically I just feel like I'm not alone."

One of the people I work with recently said that the books are like a support group between the covers of a book—you can read about other peoples' experiences and realize you're not the only one going through something.

Wright

Jack, with our *Speaking of Success* series we're trying to encourage people in our audience to be better, to live better, and be more fulfilled by reading about the experiences of our writers. Is there anyone or anything in your life that has made a difference for you and helped you to become a better person?

Canfield

Yes and we could do ten books just on that. I'm influenced by people all the time. If I were to go way back I'd have to say one of the key influences in my life was Jesse Jackson when he was still a minister in Chicago. I was teaching in an all black high school there and I went to Jesse Jackson's church with a friend one time. What happened for me was that I saw somebody with a vision. (This was before Martin Luther King was killed and Jesse was of the lieutenants in his organization.) I just saw people trying to make the world work better for a certain segment of the population. I was inspired by that kind of visionary belief that it's possible to make change.

Later on, John F. Kennedy was a hero of mine. I was very much inspired by him.

Another is a therapist by the name of Robert Resnick. He was my therapist for two years. He taught me a little formula called E + R = O that stands for Events + Response = Outcome. He said, "If you don't like your outcomes quit blaming the events and start changing your responses." One of his favorite phrases was, "If the grass on the other side of the fence looks greener, start watering your own lawn more."

I think he helped me get off any kind of self-pity I might have had because I had parents who were alcoholics. It would have been very easy to blame them for problems I might have had. They weren't very successful or rich; I was surrounded by people who were and I felt like, "God, what if I'd had parents like they had? I could have been a lot better." He just got me off that whole notion and made me realize the hand you were dealt is the hand you've got to play and take responsibility for who you are and quit complaining and blaming others and get on with your life. That was a turning point for me.

I'd say the last person who really affected me big time was a guy named W. Clement Stone who was a self-made multi-millionaire in Chicago. He taught me that success is not a four-letter word—it's nothing to be ashamed of—and you ought to go for it. He said, "The best thing you can do for the poor is not be one of them." Be a model for what it is to live a successful life. So I learned from him the principles of success and that's what I've been teaching now for more than thirty years.

Wright

He was an entrepreneur in the insurance industry, wasn't he?

Canfield

He was. He had combined insurance. When I worked for him he was worth 600 million dollars and that was before the dot.com millionaires came along in Silicon Valley. He just knew more about success. He was a good friend of Napoleon Hill (author of *Think and Grow Rich)* and he was a fabulous mentor. I really learned a lot from him.

Wright

I miss some of the men I listened to when I was a young salesman coming up and he was one of them. Napoleon Hill was another one as was Dr. Peale. All of their writings made me who I am today. I'm glad I had that opportunity.

Canfield

One speaker whose name you probably will remember, Charlie "Tremendous" Jones, says, "Who we are is a result of the books we read and the people we hang out with." I think that's so true and that's why I tell people, "If you want to have high self-esteem, hang out with people who have high self-esteem. If you want to be more spiritual, hang out with spiritual people." We're always telling our children, "Don't hang out with those kids." The reason we don't want them to is because we know how influential people are with each other. I think we need to give ourselves the same advice. Who are we hanging out with? We can hang out with them in books, cassette tapes, CDs, radio shows, and in person.

Wright

One of my favorites was a fellow named Bill Gove from Florida. I talked with him about three or four years ago. He's retired now. His mind is still as quick as it ever was. I thought he was one of the greatest speakers I had ever heard.

What do you think makes up a great mentor? In other words, are there characteristics that mentors seem to have in common?

Canfield

I think there are two obvious ones. I think mentors have to have the time to do it and the willingness to do it. I also think they need to be people who are doing something you want to do. W. Clement Stone used to tell me, "If you want to be rich, hang out with rich people. Watch what they do, eat what they eat, dress the way they dress. Try it on." He wasn't suggesting that you give up your authentic self, but he was pointing out that rich people probably have habits that you don't have and you should study them.

I always ask salespeople in an organization, "Who are the top two or three in your organization?" I tell them to start taking them out to lunch and dinner and for a drink and finding out what they do. Ask them, "What's your secret?" Nine times out of ten they'll be willing to tell you.

This goes back to what we said earlier about asking. I'll go into corporations and I'll say, "Who are the top ten people?" They'll all tell me and I'll say, "Did you ever ask them what they do different than you?"

"No," they'll reply.

"Why not?"

"Well, they might not want to tell me."

"How do you know? Did you ever ask them? All they can do is say no. You'll be no worse off than you are now."

So I think with mentors you just look at people who seem to be living the life you want to live and achieving the results you want to achieve.

What we say in our book is when that you approach a mentor they're probably busy and successful and so they haven't got a lot of time. Just ask, "Can I talk to you for ten minutes every month?" If I know it's only going to be ten minutes I'll probably say yes. The neat thing is if I like you I'll always give you more than ten minutes, but that ten minutes gets you in the door.

Wright

In the future are there any more Jack Canfield books authored singularly?

Canfield

One of my books includes the formula I mentioned earlier: E + R = O. I just felt I wanted to get that out there because every time I give a speech and I talk about that the whole room gets so quiet that you could hear a pin drop—I can tell people are really getting value. Then I'm going to do a series of books on the principles of success. I've got about 150 of them that I've identified over the years. I have a book down the road I want to do that's called *No More Put-Downs,* which is a book probably aimed mostly at parents, teacher and managers. There's a culture we have now of put-down humor. Whether it's *Married With Children* or *All in the Family,* there's that characteristic of macho put-down humor. There's research now showing how bad it is for kids' self-esteem when the coaches do it so I want to get that message out there as well.

Wright

It's really not that funny, is it?

Canfield

No, we'll laugh it off because we don't want to look like we're a wimp but underneath we're hurt. The research now shows that you're better off breaking a child's bones than you are breaking their spirit. A bone will heal much more quickly than their emotional spirit will.

Wright

I remember recently reading a survey where people listed the top five people who had influenced them. I've tried it on a couple of groups at church and in other places. In my case, and in the survey, approximately three out of the top five are always teachers. I wonder if that's going to be the same in the next decade.

Canfield

I think that's probably because as children we're at our most formative years. We actually spend more time with our teachers than we do with our parents. Research shows that the average parent only interacts verbally with each of their children only about eight and a half minutes a day. Yet at school they're interacting with their teachers for anywhere from six to eight hours depending on how long the school day is, including coaches, chorus directors, etc.

I think that in almost everybody's life there's been that one teacher who loved him or her as a human being—an individual—not just one of the many students the teacher was supposed to fill full of History and English. That teacher believed in you and inspired you.

Les Brown is one of the great motivational speakers in the world. If it hadn't been for one teacher who said, "I think you can do more than be in a special ed. class. I think you're the one," he'd probably still be cutting grass in the median strip of the highways in Florida instead of being a $35,000-a-talk speaker.

Wright

I had a conversation one time with Les. He told me about this wonderful teacher who discovered Les was dyslexic. Everybody else called him dumb and this one lady just took him under her wing and had him tested. His entire life changed because of her interest in him.

Canfield

I'm on the board of advisors of the Dyslexic Awareness Resource Center here in Santa Barbara. The reason is because I taught high school with a lot of kids who were called at-risk—kids who would end up in gangs and so forth. What we found over and over was that about 78 percent of all the kids in the juvenile detention centers in Chicago were kids who had learning disabilities—primarily dyslexia—but there were others as well. They were never diagnosed and they weren't doing well in school so they'd drop out. As soon as a student drops out of school he or she becomes subject to the influence of gangs and other kinds of criminal and drug linked activities. If these kids had been diagnosed earlier we'd get rid of a large amount of the juvenile crime in America because there are a lot of really good programs that can teach dyslexics to read and excel in school.

Wright

My wife is a teacher and she brings home stories that are heartbreaking about parents not being as concerned with their children as they used to be, or at least not as helpful as they used to be. Did you find that to be a problem when you were teaching?

Canfield

It depends on what kind of district you're in. If it's a poor district the parents could be on drugs, alcoholics, and basically just not available. If you're in a really high rent district the parents not available because they're both working, coming home tired, they're jet-setters, or they're working late at the office because they're workaholics. Sometimes it just legitimately takes two paychecks to pay the rent anymore.

I find that the majority of parents care but often they don't know what to do. They don't know how to discipline their children. They don't know how to help them with their homework. They can't pass on skills that they never acquired themselves. Unfortunately, the trend tends to be like a chain letter. The people with the least amount of skills tend to have the most number of children. The other thing is that you get crack babies (infants born addicted to crack cocaine because of the mother's addiction). In Los Angeles one out of every ten babies born is a crack baby.

Wright

That's unbelievable.

Canfield

Yes and another statistic is that by the time 50 percent of the kids are twelve years old they have started experimenting with alcohol. I see a lot of that in the Bible belt. The problem is not the big city, urban designer drugs but alcoholism. Another thing you get, unfortunately, is a lot of let's call it familial violence—kids getting beat up, parents who drink and then explode—child abuse and sexual abuse. You see a lot of that.

Wright

Most people are fascinated by these television shows about being a survivor. What has been the greatest comeback that you have made from adversity in your career or in your life?

Canfield

You know it's funny, I don't think I've had a lot of major failures and setbacks where I had to start over. My life's been on an intentional curve. But I do have a lot of challenges. Mark and I are always setting goals that challenge us. We always say, "The purpose of setting a really big goal is not so that you can achieve it so much, but it's who you become in the process of achieving it." A friend of mine, Jim Rohn, says, "You want to set goals big enough so that in the process of achieving them you become someone worth being."

I think that to be a millionaire is nice but so what? People make the money and then they lose it. People get the big houses and then they burn down, or Silicon Valley goes belly up and all of a sudden they don't have a big house anymore. But who you became in the process of learning how to do that can never be taken away from you. So what we do is constantly put big challenges in front of us.

We have a book called *Chicken Soup for the Teacher's Soul.* (You'll have to make sure to get a copy for your wife.) I was a teacher and a teacher trainer for years. But because of the success of the *Chicken Soup* books I haven't been in the education world that much. I've got to go out and relearn how do I market to that world? I met with a Superintendent of Schools. I met with a guy named Jason Dorsey who's one of the number one consultants in the world in that area. I found out who has the best selling book in that area. I sat down with his wife for a day and talked about her marketing approaches.

I believe that if you face any kind of adversity, whether losing your job, your spouse dies, you get divorced, you're in an accident like Christopher Reeves and become paralyzed, or whatever, you simply do what you have to do. You find out who's already handled the problem and how did they've handled it. Then you get the support you need to get through it by their example. Whether it's a counselor in your church or you go on a retreat or you read the Bible, you do something that gives you the support you need to get to the other end.

You also have to know what the end is that you want to have. Do you want to be remarried? Do you just want to have a job and be a single mom? What is it? If you reach out and ask for support I think you'll get help. People really like to help other people. They're not always available because sometimes they're going through problems also; but there's always someone with a helping hand.

Often I think we let our pride get in the way. We let our stubbornness get in the way. We let our belief in how the world should be interfere and get in our way instead of dealing with how the world is. When we get that out of that way then we can start doing that which we need to do to get where we need to go.

Wright

If you could have a platform and tell our audience something you feel that would help or encourage them, what would you say?

Canfield

I'd say number one is to believe in yourself, believe in your dreams, and trust your feelings. I think too many people are trained wrong when they're little kids. For example, when kids are mad at their daddy they're told, "You're not mad at your Daddy."

They say, "Gee, I thought I was."

Or the kid says, "That's going to hurt," and the doctor says, "No it's not." Then they give you the shot and it hurts. They say, "See that didn't hurt, did it?" When that happened to you as a kid, you started to not trust yourself.

You may have asked your mom, "Are you upset?" and she says, "No," but she really was. So you stop learning to trust your perception.

I tell this story over and over. There are hundreds of people I've met who've come from upper class families where they make big incomes and the dad's a doctor. The kid wants to be a mechanic and work in an auto shop because that's what he loves. The family says, "That's beneath us. You can't do that." So the kid ends up being an anesthesiologist killing three people because he's not paying attention. What he really wants to do is tinker with cars. I tell people you've got to trust your own feelings, your own motivations, what turns you on, what you want to do, what makes you feel good, and quit worrying about what other people say, think, and want for you.

Decide what you want for yourself and then do what you need to do to go about getting it. It takes work.

I read a book a week minimum and at the end of the year I've read fifty-two books. We're talking about professional books—books on self-help, finances, psychology, parenting, and so forth. At the end of ten years I've read 520 books. That puts me in the top 1 percent of people knowing important information in this country. But most people are spending their time watching television.

When I went to work for W. Clement Stone, he told me, "I want you to cut out one hour a day of television."

"Okay," I said, "what do I do with it?"

"Read," he said.

He told me what kind of books to read. He said, "At the end of a year you'll have spent 365 hours reading. Divide that by a forty-hour work week and that's nine and a half weeks of education every year."

I thought, "Wow, that's two months." It was like going back to summer school.

As a result of his advice I have close to 8,000 books in my library. The reason I'm involved in this book project instead of someone else is that people like me, Jim Rohn, Les Brown, and you read a lot. We listen to tapes and we go to seminars. That's why we're the people with the information.

I always say that your raise becomes effective when you do. You'll become more effective as you gain more skills, more insight, and more knowledge.

Wright

Jack, I have watched your career for over a decade and your accomplishments are just outstanding. But your humanitarian efforts are really what impress me. I think that you're doing great things not only in California, but all over the country.

Canfield

It's true. In addition to all of the work we do, we pick one to three charities and we've given away over six million dollars in the last eight years, along with our publisher who matches every penny we give away. We've planted over a million trees in Yosemite National Park. We've bought hundreds of thousands of cataract operations in third world countries. We've contributed to the Red Cross, the Humane Society, and on it goes. It feels like a real blessing to be able to make that kind of a contribution to the world.

Wright

Today we have been talking with Jack Canfield, founder and co-creator of the *Chicken Soup for the Soul* book series. As of 2006, there are sixty-five titles and eighty million copies in print in over thirty-seven <u>languages</u>.

Canfield

The most recent book is *The Success Principles*. In it I share sixty-four principles that other people and I have utilized to achieve great levels of success.

In 2002 we published *Chicken Soup for the Soul of America.* It includes stories that grew out of 9/11 and is a real healing book for our nation. I would encourage readers to get a copy and share it with their families.

Wright

I will stand in line to get one of those. Thank you so much being with us on *Speaking of Success.*

About The Author

JACK CANFIELD is one of America's leading experts on developing self-esteem and peak performance. A dynamic and entertaining speaker, as well as a highly sought-after trainer, he has a wonderful ability to inform and inspire audiences toward developing their own human potential and personal effectiveness.

Jack Canfield is most well-known for the *Chicken Soup for the Soul* series, which he co-authored with Mark Victor Hansen, and for his audio programs about building high self-esteem. Jack is the founder of Self-Esteem Seminars, located in Santa Barbara, California, which trains entrepreneurs, educators, corporate leaders, and employees how to accelerate the achievement of their personal and professional goals. Jack is also the founder of The Foundation for Self Esteem, located in Culver City, California, which provides self-esteem resources and training to social workers, welfare recipients, and human resource professionals.

Jack graduated from Harvard in 1966, received his ME degree at the university of Massachusetts in 1973, and earned an Honorary Doctorate from the University of Santa Monica. He has been a high school and university teacher, a workshop facilitator, a psychotherapist, and a leading authority in the area of self-esteem and personal development.

As a result of his work with prisoners, welfare recipients, and inner-city youth, Jack was appointed by the state legislature to the California Task Force to Promote Self-Esteem and Personal and Social Responsibility. He also served on the board of trustees of the National Council for Self-Esteem.

Jack Canfield
Worldwide Headquarters
The Jack Canfield Companies
P.O. Box 30880
Santa Barbara, CA 93130
Phone: 805.563.2935
Fax: 805.563.2945
www.jackcanfield.com

Chapter 11

GREG SMITH

David Wright (Wright)
Today we're talking with Greg Smith. Greg was born with muscular dystrophy. In 2005 his remarkable life story was revealed to America in a PBS documentary, *On A Roll,* and in his autobiography, *On A Roll: Reflections from America's Wheelchair Dude with the Winning Attitude.* He's founder and eleven-year host of *On a Roll—Talk Radio on Life and Disability,* a syndicated program that is aired on over seventy stations nationwide. Since 2003 he has hosted *The Strength Coach,* a syndicated radio show that has made the leap to television. He has given hundreds of keynote addresses, teaching audiences how to build inner strength.

Greg, welcome to *Speaking of Success*.

Greg Smith (Smith)
Thank you.

Wright

How has living your entire life with muscular dystrophy made you a stronger person?

Smith

Every day of my life I'm getting physically weaker. Accepting that limitation has given me no choice but to focus on the positive things in life. I look at the potential that exists when I ignore my restrictions. I have no choice but to do this if I want to remain positive and productive.

Wright

What have been some of the obstacles you have had to overcome?

Smith

Obviously my physical challenges have been very extreme and continue to present great obstacles on a daily basis. But those obstacles have given me the strength to face another, more daunting challenge: the low expectations of other people.

So many times in my life, I have not been given opportunities because people didn't think I could do things. In my work life I haven't been promoted to the level that I aspired to because employers had a fear that I would be less productive on the job or that others would feel awkward in my presence because of my wheelchair. But I've always found a way around these limitations and problems.

In my career I found a way to start my own business, which allowed me to succeed without worrying about the limiting beliefs of others, including the limiting beliefs of a boss. I think that with every obstacle there has come a creative way to reach around it and solve the problem. Every single day in my life I've overcome severe obstacles. Some of them are physical. These days even climbing in and out of my wheelchair is very difficult but I have found ways to do that both physically and creatively with seeking help and in other ways.

If you live a life of daily extreme challenges you'll end up devising creative ways to achieve your goals and make your dreams come true.

Wright

Most people would look at a person like you with a sense of pity and feel that you are unfortunate. How are you fortunate?

Smith

We are all sensitive beings and can interpret the smallest human reactions. I sense on a daily basis that assumptions are being made about my lifestyle from a single fleeting glance. People see the wheelchair and the severity of my disability and immediately assume that my life is only half and that I'm unfortunate to be in my condition. Obviously I'm quite disabled; I can't sit upright in my wheelchair without using a Velcro strap around my chest. I can no longer reach above the level of my shoulders because my arms are weakening. It would be easy for me to write an entire chapter about the progression of my disability and new limitations I must accept every year. Part of my condition is that it's gradually worsening

To say all that and then to say I wouldn't trade places with anybody might seem to be an unbelievable statement. But the truth of that statement is based on the fact that I'm privileged. I'm very fortunate to have a lot of the things I do enjoy in my life. I have three wonderful children. I can still drive in an adapted mini-van so I'm always on the go to speaking engagements or to watch my children play sports. And I travel around the country experiencing the thrill of inspiring and motivating people. I'm earning a great living from my speaking career. I'm an author and a nationally syndicated broadcaster. All of these things combined allow me to live a different life than most would expect and one that's quite rewarding.

I think that to assume anything about others is a mistake. You might look at some people who are physically attractive and physically healthy and assume they are happy and well adjusted. But those people may have more severe disabilities internally than I do externally. I think I am blessed with a lot of inner strength to be able to overcome my physical weaknesses. This allows me to encourage others and that's a fortunate place to be.

Wright

How does your perspective about your life and your situation help others?

Smith

I have a deep seated belief that I was given a special mission in life. It is a mission I'm grateful to have been selected to carry out. It is a twofold mission—to inspire and to enlighten.

I inspire people by making them realize they can ignore their limitations and focus on their abilities to achieve a level of self-worth.

Speaking of Success

I enlighten people by showing them that individuals with very severe disabilities can be civically engaged and active, productive, successful, happy citizens. I'm fortunate to be able to look at the world through a different lens and to report and to write and speak and broadcast about the lessons I've learned that can be helpful to other people.

Wright
What would you suggest to people that would give them a state of mind open to success?

Smith
Success and failure are internally determined. We can be successful or not as a result of our own attitudes about life and about where we believe we should be. Fundamentally, many people do not accept their current situation. They have aspiration but they don't have acceptance of where they are. I think it's important to acknowledge where you are "on the field" and how far you have to go. A lot of people want to deny that the bad aspects of life exist. You look to the positive but you can't do that without acknowledging where you are and being realistic about it.

Another important thing is to realize you can't do it by yourself. You have to look to your teammates in order to get support. We live in a very interdependent society. We have successes and failures based on the responses we get from our teammates—our family, our friends, our spiritual mentors, and those who are alongside of us in our profession. Surround yourself with a winning team to keep that positive state in your mind.

Following your purpose is also important. Many people go through life aimlessly without realizing that their specific life has a very specific purpose. To uncover that and follow it is definitely a key to success.

To be successful, we need inner strength. In the physical world, it takes strength to lift weights. Life's challenges are like weights. To keep a positive attitude, we must lift the weights of life's challenges. But to begin that daunting task, we need to feed our mind the right diet every day. If we didn't nourish our bodies daily, we would weaken physically to the point of death. We must have nutrition to build strength. To be successful, we must build our inner strength. To build inner strength, our diet must include positive reading materials, positive tapes or CDs, and encouraging words from teammates.

150

The key is to keep that nourishment going into your mind on a daily basis. It can be just a little bit every day but to overcome the negativity that exists in our society we need to do that. It is important to read books like this one and listen to programs and CDs that will provide that nourishment.

Another way is to exercise mentally. We must look at challenges as exercises and lift the weights of life's challenges. We must embrace the knowledge that there will be weights to lift every day and we need to face that fact with enthusiasm. We need to seek out and take on the weights of life's challenges every day. The more difficult things we do, the more success we have and the more confidence we gain.

We can immerse ourselves in the positive and achieve some results in the face of difficulty, however, in order to see major life change, we need to develop our discipline. We must realize that it is within our basic human nature to go in the path of least resistance and to stay within our comfort zone of behavior. But if we can force ourselves to do difficult things over an extended period of time, it will build our confidence and our inner strength.

When we have achieved familiarity with positive results, we find ourselves "in the zone." That means in a state of repetitive success. We can have one success and feel pretty good about it but if we have two in a row then that leads to a feeling of confidence and the ability to move forward and expect success.

Wright

What kinds of habits can people develop that will lead to building inner strength?

Smith

It takes twenty-one days to establish a habit. If we can do the diet and exercise for twenty-one days we'll have developed the expectation of success through inner strength. It's important to do positive things long enough that they become second nature. At first they'll seem difficult but the more you do them, the easier they'll get and pretty soon they become standard practice.

Wright

How is discipline an important ingredient to building inner strength?

Smith

There are a couple of definitions of discipline. One is remaining true to a regimen—to a program. It's important to do that to establish it as a habit.

Another type of discipline is sticking with one particular problem until it's resolved. It can be something very important or it can be insignificant. But I think any success that comes from discipline can inspire you to new levels of success.

I have a story I like to tell about this. I am very weak in my hands. I was home alone one evening and I ordered a pizza and a two-liter Pepsi. When the pizza and Pepsi were delivered I wasn't thinking about what I was supposed to be doing. I paid for the pizza and the delivery guy set it in my lap. I went to the table and opened the box, took a couple of bites and realized I'd made a terrible mistake. I couldn't open a two-liter container of Pepsi with my hands—my fingers aren't strong enough to grab the cap and twist it with enough force to open it.

At that point I was faced with a decision: settling for water or remaining determined to enjoy the Pepsi. Once I made the decision to have Pepsi, the discipline began.

I thought of several different ways I could try to get the cap off. One of the things I tried was to run hot water on it and use a towel to expand the strength of my grip. I spent about twenty minutes but I couldn't get it open that way. Then I tried getting some duct tape and drum sticks to use as a lever. I spent another probably thirty minutes with scissors and tape and sticks trying to construct this carefully designed lever system but the tape broke.

About an hour into this effort I decided that what I needed to get were tools. I went to my garage and I got a pair of pliers and a wrench. I put all my weight and strength into the pliers and I thought I was making progress in twisting the cap. All I had done was put horizontal scratches on the vertical ridges on the plastic cap. I was getting frustrated but I'd made a promise to myself to have soda not water. So I went back to my garage looking for something else and out of frustration threw the tools toward the direction of my toolbox. They missed and slid over to a remote corner of the garage. I looked down and out of the corner of my eye, I spotted the solution!

I rolled back into the kitchen armed with a dart from my dart board! I stabbed this two-liter Pepsi and was able to squeeze out the best tasting lukewarm beverage I've ever had in my life.

This was a very insignificant thing that happened to me but when I lifted that weight and stepped into that challenge it gave me a lot of strength and confidence in the fact that no matter what situation arises, there's always a strong possibility I'm going to be successful. I think this is an important part of discipline that has come from my disability I can explain and teach others—sticking with the problem and having the confidence knowing you can solve it.

Wright

That's obviously an important part of willing yourself to win. This leads us to our next question: why win?

Smith

I think victory leads to other victories, not only to yourself but for the people you love—setting a good example for your family and your friends by being victorious as opposed to being defeated. We often feel down and out and we look for ways to solve a certain problem. It's okay to admit when we're not winning and to seek out suggestions from others about ways to win.

It's important to have a dedication and a focus on victory in everything in life, not only in financial and career success but in serving your mission, whatever your mission is. You may lose a lot of battles that take place outside of your mission and your goal but as long as you are reaching out and doing what you're supposed to be doing with your life then you've won.

Another thing is you're not going to win all of them. You're not going to win in every aspect of your life but keep in mind that the aspects you are winning are giving you validity and making you someone who is important in this world. Don't allow yourself to be brought down by areas in your life where you're not victorious. Its okay to seek out victory in those areas but don't let that overshadow your success in other areas—in ones that are more focused on your purpose.

Wright

You touched on the failure aspect of that answer. What do you mean by "familiarity with failure"?

Smith

You're not going to be 100 percent successful and victorious in life. In fact, you're probably going to be less victorious in life than you will be victorious. There will be a lot of failure in life. Becoming familiar with failure enables you to feel that it's not so painful to lose, which will give you more strength to try. If you're familiar with the fact that you're going to fail and you don't let it get you down, then that will give you strength for victory.

So to me, familiarity with failure means accepting the fact that most of the time things are not going to go right. But the few times that things do go right, they're going to have a big impact on you and others.

Wright

How do you rationalize the undisputable fact that you are rapidly getting weaker due to muscular dystrophy and your longevity is uncertain?

Smith

I have lived my entire life with limited life-span expectations. When I was born, doctors told my parents that I would not live past my teens. When I was a teenager, I was given a death watch in my mid-to-late twenties. In actuality, my late twenties is when I started having children! I think that limited life-span expectations have forced me to try to seek out as much success, victory, love, and happiness in a more rapid way. I'm very inspired to live the rest of my days in ways that are enjoyable but in ways that will impact the people I love.

Yes, I'm getting weaker and it's difficult and frustrating at times to know that I can no longer do certain things. For example, I can't raise my hands high enough to turn the lights on and off anymore, so we're going to have to lower the light switches. I could go on and on about things like that such as traveling independently or using a public restroom. But I understand that I'm weaker and I do have muscular dystrophy and there's nothing I can do about that. I also understand that I have a lot of strength left and I have a lot of passion and energy to reach my goals and live my purpose. In a lot of ways the fact that I'm getting weaker inspires me more to take on challenges and to move toward my goals in life and my purpose.

It is also a unique twist to realize that getting weaker is an advantage. There's a country song titled, "Live Like You Were Dying," written by Tim McGraw. That song resonates with me because my uncertain longevity gives me a lot of fuel to go fast and to live in a way that I deserve to live the rest of my life. My longevity is uncertain but my success and happiness and productivity are certain. In fact, I'm very proud of the fact that if I died today I would still be remembered for being a person who made a difference in this world. So the more I can cram into whatever time I have left and really change the world in a special way, the happier I'll feel when the time comes.

Wright

What do you want to do with your life and how does it help others to have a mission and a purpose?

Smith

I just want to help people understand that they can overcome their limitations. I also want to help people realize and appreciate the awesome strength in the disability community. We can all learn from that strength.

I am now making a transition from radio to television, creating programming that helps people see a lot of these limitations we face and gives them some inspiration to achieve their own goals and purpose. The media is an important catalyst of what we as a society believe and feel and what our attitudes are. If people with disabilities can move into the mass media and really have a place in America's living rooms where we can be seen and accepted as equals or as people who have special talents, then that will be a positive thing.

I'd like to continue to speak and write and reach out with my message. I would also like to shine the mass media spotlight on myself and others who have a similar mission and purpose. My goal now is to move forward in the mass media.

Wright

What an interesting conversation. I appreciate your taking this time to answer these questions. I wish you continued success in what you are doing.

Today we've been talking with Greg Smith. He is founder and eleven-year host of *On a Roll—Talk Radio on Life and Disability,* a syndicated program that is aired on over seventy stations nationwide. Since 2003 he has hosted *The Strength Coach,* a syndicated radio show that has made the leap to television. He has given hundreds of keynote addresses, teaching audiences how to build inner strength.

Thank you for being with us, Greg, on *Speaking of Success.*

About the Author

GREG SMITH is "America's Strength Coach." When you envision the word, "strength," you probably don't think of a sixty-five-pound man in a power wheelchair. How could a "Strength Coach" be so frail? Then, suddenly, you "get it." Moments into his presentation, after hearing his resonant voice, you find yourself realizing that his presence reveals a deeper level of strength—*inner strength!*

Born with muscular dystrophy, raised by a football coach, Greg's inner strength message is woven into all of his programs: "In any situation, great opportunity exists for victory." Greg's remarkable life story was revealed to America in a PBS documentary film, *On A Roll: Family, Disability, and the American Dream,* which aired in February, 2005. His autobiography, *On A Roll: Reflections from America's Wheelchair Dude with the Winning Attitude,* hit the bookshelves in May 2005. His radio show, *The Strength Coach*, airs nationwide on the Radio America Network. For eleven years, Greg hosted *On A Roll—Talk Radio on Life and Disability,* a syndicated program that aired on more than seventy stations nationwide.

Greg has been honored as an "Exceptional American" by the National Liberty Museum in Philadelphia, profiled in the *Wall Street Journal, New York Times, New York Times Magazine,* CBS News, and National Public Radio. He is a member of the National Speakers Association and makes dozens of trips across the country to address corporate, academic, and private audiences. In addition to his busy career, he is the father of three active children.

Greg Smith
On A Roll Communications
3624 Perryman Road
Ocean Springs, MS 39564
Phone: 877.331.7563
E-mail: greg@TheStrengthCoach.com
www.TheStrengthCoach.com

Chapter 12

BRAD WORTHLEY

David Wright (Wright)

Today we are talking with Brad Worthley. Brad is an accomplished business consultant with over thirty-two years of management experience. He is internationally acclaimed as a leadership and customer service expert and has trained hundreds of thousands of people in a wide range of industries throughout the world. He teaches businesses how to consistently build and retain both customer and employee loyalty by changing their culture and not just their people. Brad is an author, consultant, and trainer who works with small and medium sized companies up to some of the largest corporations in the world.

In his spare time he has volunteered as a youth soccer, baseball, and basketball coach for the last fifteen years and he volunteers weekly at a domestic violence shelter where he works with children. He has a son in the Army who, as of this printing, is flying unmanned spy planes, called drones, in Iraq in an effort to protect our troops.

Brad, welcome to *Speaking of Success.*

Brad Worthley (Worthley)

Thanks, David.

Wright

You use the word "culture" throughout your Web site and on your products. Why is that word so important?

Worthley

So many organizations have been making the same mistake for hundreds of years. Anytime they introduce something new to their employees, especially when it has to do with customer service or sales, they introduce it and use the word "program." They go to the employees and say, "We've got a new customer service program." Here is the problem: I did employee surveys a few years back and found out that the perception of most employees is that a program has an expiration date of about ninety days. So when you tell employees that you have a new customer service program, the employee flips a switch in his or her brain that says, "Oh, it has an expiration date— it's going away in ninety days so why should I jump on board?" And of course it gets replaced by another program when the organization loses enthusiasm for the previous one.

This happens with both sales and service. It tends to be a swinging pendulum because leaders in the organization will say, "We've got a new customer service program," and then a few months later they'll admit they forgot about sales, then they will go back and create a sales program. So this pendulum swings back and forth and unfortunately it impacts their employees as far as their buy-in is concerned. Then, many organizations come to realize that the word "program" is ineffective and they became aware of the message that it sent, so they replaced it with the word "initiative," which was not a whole lot better (that one lasts about ninety-one days).

When we use the word "culture," it means that sales and service are woven deep within the fabric of the organization. When employees hear the word "culture," they know it's not going away. It's not going to be temporary. When you hear the word "culture," you're going to hear it attached to organizations like Nordstrom, Ritz Carlton, or Disney. These are organizations that are passion driven and they've all got great service cultures. If you were going to go to work at Nordstrom, Ritz Carlton, or Disney, you know you are going to be held to a higher standard because that's what the word "culture" indicates.

As leaders we have to be very careful because the words we use can actually be interpreted differently by employees and it can change their buy-in. If we change our vocabulary just slightly, we can sometimes change our culture dramatically.

Wright

How does an organization create a culture and not just another program?

Worthley

Upper management needs to be totally committed and passionate about it. Leaders need to really walk the walk and talk the talk. Whenever I am working with CEOs or upper management, I try to get them to understand they are like a conductor. They've got a baton in their hand and they are moving the baton back and forth just as though they've got an orchestra in front of them. The slower they move, the slower the entire organization moves; the faster they move, the faster the organization moves.

In a leader's position, his or her job is to walk into the organization and create energy. When leaders walk in a room they are either going to give it energy and bring everybody up, or they are going to drain their people of energy and bring everybody down.

In my previous company, called Genesis Group, I had thirty-five full-time employees. Every time I went to grab the doorknob to walk into the office I ran this thought through my head, "Lights, camera, action!" I opened up the door and my job was to walk in and feed my employees energy. That was my job; that's what I was paid to do. I'm still paid to give people energy when I am doing training seminars or keynotes.

Regardless of whether a leader is going through trauma such as a divorce, a car accident, arguments with family members, or any of the other events that can create personal anxiety, he or she has to leave it at the door. I am not saying it is easy, but if you are a leader, when you walk through the office door, your job is to put aside what happens outside the office, focus on your duty as a leader of people, and inspire and motivate your employees. Even if something happens within your business walls, your behavior in reaction to the issue may impact everyone around you. If a "fire" flares up—a problem or emergency—you can either throw a bucket of gas on the fire, which quickly escalates the problem, or you can throw a bucket of water on it to quickly extinguish it.

In leadership, we need to change our behavior first if we expect our employees to change their behavior. There's a *huge* difference between managers and leaders, but unfortunately the majority of the people I see in supervisory roles in the world today tend to be managers. Managers are number-makers and leaders are people-makers. Managers tend to be short-term thinkers and leaders are long-term thinkers. Managers are reactive to situations while leaders are more proactive. Managers think they have all the answers, while leaders have great questions. Managers are prone to want to control people, while leaders like to empower people. Managers like to maintain the status quo and keep things the way they are and leaders embrace change and like to invent a new future.

We have created managers because we take employees who are really good at their duties and we want to show them our appreciation, so we promote them up to a management role. Then we teach them how to manage keys, how to manage inventory, how to manage payroll, how to manage supplies, and how to manage this and that. What we end up with are managers instead of leaders. We don't have people who have been taught how to inspire and motivate people.

If you think about the word itself, the question comes to mind: does anyone want to be "managed"? Of course not! And nobody I know wants to be "bossed." However, we use the word "manager" and we use the word "boss" frequently. These are probably two of our most common terms for supervisors, even though they can be perceived negatively.

Another disservice we do to those we promote into management roles is that we give them roles they are not prepared to handle— they've usually had no leadership training at all. This is really sad because we are throwing them into the fire and asking them to perform these duties before we've given them any training for their role as leaders.

Specific leadership training and proactive development for the up and comers is absolutely critical to organizations, but most organizations just don't do it. I wish that organizations would spend more time filling up the pipeline with employees who have stepped forward and said, "You know what, I'm interested in becoming a leader someday." We need to find these people and begin to develop them early on so that when we do have a position open up, we can look into our pipeline and see those who have embraced the leadership role the most and have exhibited those kinds of behaviors. When we move them into the role, they are already trained and ready to go. But that truly doesn't happen out there in the real world very often.

This is further supported by a survey I did of my monthly newsletter readers in August of 2006. These people represent many different industries throughout the world. I asked them this question: "Does your organization have a formal leadership development program in place to create great leaders?" The response was 13 percent said "Yes" and 87 percent said "No."

Managers also tend to be trainers, while leaders know how to coach their people. Training is a one-time event that tells people what to do, which leaves employees sometimes feeling dictated to. Coaching is a process that is continuous and consistent. Additionally, we explain to our employees why they need to change or why this behavior change request is better for them or the organization. Coaching is a softer and kinder form of communicating with employees that inspires and motivates positive change.

Coaching is about deepening an employee's learning and forwarding the actions he or she is trying to achieve. When employees come to us with questions or problems, we should ask them to try to solve them for themselves and come to us with recommendations, but most managers don't do that. Managers tend to give them the answers because they think it will save time. Managers know that it might take ten or fifteen minutes to stop work and show them how to find the answer for themselves or coach them. Answering the question or giving them the answer only takes a few seconds so managers fool themselves into thinking that giving them answers is the best thing for everyone involved. Unfortunately, this is a tremendous disservice to employees because they are robbed of learning how to think for themselves. They are also robbed of the gratification of coming up with answers themselves, which is very unfair.

Being a great coach is not about having all the right answers, it's about having the right questions. It's like walking through a park. You're side by side with an employee and you come to a "Y" in the path but you don't tell him or her which way to go, you ask the right questions in order to help *the employee* determine the best path to take. That's like the old saying, "If you give them a fish you can feed them for a day, but if you teach them how to fish you can feed them for a lifetime."

Coaching dialogue is completely different than managing dialogue. As an example, a "manager" type of dialogue would be the following scenario: The manager observes an employee handling an angry customer in a negative way. The manager might say something like, "I observed your interaction with that customer and he walked away unhappy. What did you do to him?" Once the employee explains what happened, the manager might say, "I don't ever want you to do that again. So the next time, either treat customers better or come get me and I'll handle it." That's the way a manager might handle the situation.

A leader who wants to coach the employee might say, "I observed your interaction with that customer and was left with the perception that he walked away unhappy. How did you feel about the interaction?" The leader will let the employee talk through it and deepen his or her learning about the experience. Then the leader might say, "If you could back up time and do it all over again, what might you do differently to make a more positive outcome for everybody?" Once again, the leader will give the employee a lot of time to think through it and then listen to the employee's recommendations. The leader would then acknowledge the employee for thinking through the situation properly and coming up with new ideas on how to handle it.

If the leader would like to contribute some additional ideas to make it easier for the employee to handle the situation better next time or to enhance the customer's experience even more, the leader might make suggestions to the employee using the following dialogue: "May I offer you some additional thoughts on how we might exceed the customer's expectations in that situation?" Then the leader will wait for the employee to say "Yes," because now he or she has been invited into the employee's world. The employee shouldn't feel dictated to when the leader simply said, "May I offer you?" and the employee replies, "Yes."

So coaching is really a softer form of communication that helps develop far better employees and reduces anxiety between employees and their supervisors.

Wright

Why do you think it's so important for leadership to change first?

Worthley

Statistically we have been able to prove that customer service training alone will not stick if leadership has not undergone specialized training on how to lead people in a service culture.

Back in 1991 when I owned Genesis Group, we performed "mystery shopping" as one of our services. We began working with a very large nationwide bank. They had us perform what is called a "baseline mystery shop" (sometimes it's called a "baseline secret shop"). They wanted to find out how productive their employees were at the time and what level of service they are offering before any training occurs. Then they had us go out immediately afterward and do customer service and sales training.

Within thirty days after the training was complete we went out and mystery shopped again to find out how effective the training was, and it was pretty impressive. They averaged a 45 percent increase in overall employee productivity. We were all just thrilled that the training seemed to have been effective. One month after that, we mystery shopped again and got an additional 5 percent increase. The month after that we shopped again and got a further 3 percent increase. Then all of a sudden, at about the fourth month, we saw stagnation. The employee's productivity and increased level of performance just stopped.

The next month (the fifth month), productivity scores actually decreased for a few consecutive months thereafter in small increments. Even though they didn't revert back to their original old scores, they still had deterioration that we could not understand. This happened with every single customer for almost a two-year period. So we performed employee surveys to try to figure out why this was happening. The employees reported that the customers were not very good at responding when they did something new. As an example, when employees used the customer's name, the customer did not show any immediate response or signs of gratification. Also, the supervisors were not patting the employees on the back or giving them any praise or recognition for their behavior change. Therefore, the employees just reverted back to their old behaviors because it seemed that no one cared.

Immediately after that employee feedback, I developed a training seminar titled "Outstanding Leadership in a Service Culture." The entire design of that training was focused on how leaders can change their behavior just slightly in order to dramatically impact the people they lead.

All of our new clients went through almost the same process as previous clients, starting with the baseline mystery shop. However, this time, before we did the sales and customer service training, we did the new leadership training first. We saw the same immediate increase in scores as before, which was great. Thirty days later we saw another small increase in the mystery shop scores, sixty days a little bit more, and ninety days a little more. The wonderful thing is that we were able to sustain that growth for about twelve to eighteen months before we saw any stagnation and it was pretty rare to see deterioration.

What we learned is that the leader plays a dramatic role in not only building, but also in sustaining a service culture.

Wright

What else can leaders do in addition to changing their behavior to help support a service culture?

Worthley

That's a great question. Most organizations hold meeting after meeting talking about how to create more customer value. However, I encourage leaders to consider having meetings about increasing employee value. They should sit down with employees and let them know that they want them there twenty years from now, so what would it take to make that happen? The important thing is that if you are going to have a discussion like that, you want to put money aside. You want to let them know that the discussion is about creating more value but money is not going to be included in this discussion. The reason money is excluded is this: what happens when you give employees more money? Eventually they will want what? More money! So that's not going to change and we know that. This does not mean you may never have a conversation about wages, but that conversation would come later.

The key is to have open dialogue and find out what things would allow employees to enjoy their jobs more. What are the things that are going to motivate them to work harder and enjoy their work environment more? And actually, I have found over time that most of the things they request are very simplistic. They want more training, they want to be listened to, they want more praise and recognition, or they might want upgraded uniforms or equipment. Many want to be more professional and to feel that the organization is investing in their future. I found out that the feedback is actually really positive for the organizations because the employees simply want to be more active in the decisions about their work environment and they want the organization to be more successful as well.

I am also a huge believer in doing annual employee satisfaction surveys because if we want employees to be happier and more satisfied with their jobs, we need to keep measuring that. You cannot manage what you cannot measure, so employee surveys provide a great tool to organizations. You need to watch employee satisfaction levels because if the level drops at any given time, you can be certain that eventually it is going to impact the customers' experience as well.

Wright

In addition to the people part of the business, what else is required to create and sustain the service culture?

Worthley

I believe that boundaries not clearly defined are painful. And I don't mean just for the employees but for both employees and leadership. How can employees stay within boundaries if they are not clearly defined for them in writing? Every organization should have clearly defined written job descriptions for every single position in the organization and employees should actually be the ones to keep job descriptions up to date.

Job descriptions are going to change over time. They are not created once and never touched again. They need to be updated on a regular basis, and who is better to keep them up to date than the employees themselves? The skill components are not the only elements to be kept current. In addition to updating skills that are required, the behavior component should also be continually updated. For example, is the telephone to be answered before the third ring or the fourth? If it is decided that the telephone must be answered in three rings, make sure that rule is in the job description of everyone who is responsible for answering the telephone. How long should it take before a customer coming through the front door is greeted? Is it going to be twenty seconds or thirty seconds? Whatever is decided, make sure it is in print and clearly understood.

I believe that if employees understand what their boundaries are, that will make it a much more comfortable work environment for everybody. I call those non-negotiable service standards. I think we need to call them "non-negotiable" so employees understand that these things are not up for negotiation. They are not options—they are things that every single employee is required to do. I even highly recommend organizations put them onto a single sheet of paper so they are clearly defined and easy to read, then have each employee sign, date them, and put them in his or her personnel file. If they are hidden inside of a policy and procedure manual, I guarantee that most employees aren't going to remember them because there is too much else to read and retain.

When I raised my son, I created dialogue with him about things that are negotiable and non-negotiable. When he would come home from school, the non-negotiable standard was that he would *always* do his homework before he played. So he knew that when he came home he wasn't going to try to argue or debate it—he knew what he had to do. However, if he wanted to ask, "Dad, I want to stay up until ten-thirty tonight because there is a special television program on airplanes that I want to watch," I would say, "You know what, that is negotiable and it's okay with me."

I think it's important to get employees involved *in* the process of change so that they don't feel like victims *of* the change. With that in mind, I think creating a customer service committee is a great tool to help organizations create and sustain strong service cultures. You might gather about six or seven employees in a room on a monthly basis and meet for about two hours to talk about some of the things the organization can do to improve customer service. The committee's duties might include reviewing mystery shop results, employee satisfaction surveys, and customer satisfaction surveys. The goal would be to try to decide what they can do to help improve the customers' experience and get other employees involved in that process. You want to encourage innovation and out-of-the box thinking from this committee.

I think employees really have a lot of great ideas if leaders would develop a culture that would allow that kind of dialogue to occur. I also believe that employees who are challenged in their work—being pushed a little bit and stretched just a little bit beyond their boundaries—are happier employees in the long run.

Wright

Does a company's hiring practices have to change in order to achieve a service culture?

Worthley

Absolutely. Many organizations have the wrong employees in the wrong jobs and then leaders wonder why their employees are not performing; that's the fault of leadership. Many organizations struggle with making the transition to a service culture because they have placed employees in the wrong jobs or they simply hired the wrong people the first time. Many companies make desperate hiring decisions just to fill positions with warm bodies. That hiring practice will come back and haunt them. If leaders want a service culture, they must get away from the idea of hiring out of desperation and make a more diligent effort to hire properly the first time.

Some turnover is going to occur in a transition to a service culture. However, I find that sometimes turnover is healthy. There are some people who don't like change or don't want to work in a service culture and they shouldn't be there. Not everybody is created or wired to want to serve customers and if they are not, it doesn't make them bad people, they just shouldn't be working in your culture.

I would encourage every organization to telephone interview prospective employees for their first interview, especially if the employee will be on the telephone on a frequent basis. Any employee who answers and communicates by telephone in your organization is your ambassador. Obviously, there are some jobs that are much more "ambassador-like" on the telephone such as call centers or salespeople, but I think telephone interviews are crucial for many positions. If you don't like a prospective employee's telephone voice, chances are the customer is not going to like it either (the internal or external customer).

I have been preaching for twenty-five or more years, "Hire the smile and train the skill," because you cannot train people to smile. I would encourage those who have the potential to recruit new employees to carry business cards with them wherever they go. If they are at a restaurant and have a great server, they should hand that server a business card and say, "I'd like to interview you for a job." They should be a constant recruiter. Steal employees from other businesses if they are great. It's all legal and it's all fair game. In these situations you get to see employees in their real work world. You get the best interview possible because you have the chance to actually see them in action, which is not an opportunity normally available to you.

Before you hire, I would highly recommend pre-employment testing of each final candidate. I am not suggesting you test every employee who applies, but only the ones you have narrowed down as finalists.

On my Web site, which is www.BradWorthley.com, I have a customer service pre-employment test, a sales pre-employment test, and a leadership pre-employment test. These three incredible tests allow you to look inside employees' heads and see about seventeen of their personality characteristics such as agreeableness, assertiveness, emotional stability, empathy, extroversion, integrity, orderliness, work drive, teamwork, and other critical areas. These tests will provide you with many of the things that may not come out during an interview. Some people interview well but you might not find out as much as you really need to know to make the best hiring decision. The pre-employment tests not only evaluate the personality characteristics of each person, they also do something very unique—they measure the prospective employee's cognitive skills, which are more about how smart the person is. The tests look at numeric reasoning, verbal reasoning, and abstract reasoning. They also provide suggested second interview questions based on the applicant's weaknesses, which is very helpful when trying to narrow down your final selection.

It's almost crazy to not invest a few dollars on employees you'd like to have work for you for fifteen or twenty years. It's especially important to get the right people the first time which is even more critical.

Wright

Once you have the right employees in the right job, how can you increase their chance for success in their jobs?

Worthley

Well, this might sound self-serving because it is my business, but the answer to that question is training. Almost every employee survey I do for organizations, employees respond with the request for more training. They want their organizations to invest in them. As Zig Ziglar once said, "The only thing worse than training an employee and losing them, is to not train them and to keep them." The message to employees about training is, "My organization is willing to invest in my future." That is really an important thing for employees if you want them to stick around and be committed to your organization for the long-term. I think it is funny because I have leaders in organizations who say they don't want to invest money in training because their employee turnover is so high they think it would be a waste of money. Are you kidding me? That's probably *why* they have the high employee turnover! If leaders are not willing to invest in their people, those employees are not going to stick around.

I find it odd that in many industries and organizations, the employees who are on the front line are paid the least and are also the least trained. If you look at retail sales clerks, tellers, cashiers, call center agents, and many other positions, you'll realize that the remuneration is less than that of other employees. They are given the least amount of training, however, they are considered to be their company's number one ambassadors. In many organizations, these people represent 95 percent of the customers' interactions. I think that's really sad. I believe we need to invest more in our ambassadors.

Wright

Why is it that employees sometimes don't do what you ask them to do even though they have been trained?

Worthley

Training is somewhere between a science and an art form and it's taken way too lightly. I am asked from time to time if I offer on-line training and the answer is "No." The reason is that customer service and leadership, which is what I focus on, are primarily about behavior and not necessarily about skill. I'm not saying that you can do these jobs without skill—you certainly have to have skill as well—but if you write down a list of characteristics that make a great customer service employee or a great leader, you are going to find that about 80 percent of those characteristics are behaviors. So 80 percent of the characteristics we all believe make great employees are behaviors and about 20 percent of those are skill.

Yet most internal employee training is skill-based, which on-line training is great for. I think on-line training is a fabulous tool for skill-based training, but I don't think it is *as* effective for behavior modification. As a matter of fact, I created an exclusive training technique called Perception Awareness Training. I've been working on this for about twelve years. It incorporates all the critical adult learning techniques into one process, and here they are:

First, humor is an absolutely critical component to training. It is very important to use it frequently throughout training. The reason is that humor releases endorphins into the brain that attach themselves to the same receptor cells as morphine. So it's a real feel-good that keeps your brain active and it keeps your Reticular Activating System opened and retaining information.

Your brain is very powerful and can help you learn or it can inhibit you, depending on the messages it is receiving. As an example: If you set your hand on the hot burner of a stove, it sends a signal up to your brain that says, "This is painful." Your brain sends a signal back to your hand that says, "Stop the pain," so you remove your hand. Now, if you're sitting in a class or listening to a seminar and it's boring or someone is talking over your head and confusing you, your brain says, "This is painful," and sends a signal that shuts down your listening (the Reticular Activating System) in an effort to try to stop the pain. So it's really important to make sure training sessions incorporate humor or at least keep them entertaining to keep people active and learning.

Great trainers also need to be passionate about their subject matter. Have you ever gone to a seminar and listened to Zig Ziglar, Tony Robbins, or some of the other great speakers out there and when the seminar was finished you ran to the back of the room and bought as many CDs and DVDs as you could? Ask yourself what was it about that speaker that inspired you or motivated you to do that? You'll hear one common word—passion. They were passionate about what they were speaking on and they got you passionate about it as well with their behavior. So when you are in front of your employees, it is absolutely critical to make sure they feel that you are passionate about whatever it is you are trying to communicate.

Being a great storyteller is also important. I believe people don't remember statistics but they do remember great stories. I consider myself a great storyteller because ten years after attending my seminars I have had people say that they remember one of the stories I told. As long as the stories are applicable to the subject, it's great to have frequent stories to help make your point.

You also have to have powerful content in order to keep people engaged. You have to have something in there that makes them think, "Wow, I didn't know that!" You can't preach the same stuff over and over again or they will feel dictated to or lectured to. So you truly have to have powerful content that keeps them inspired and motivated. You can gather powerful content by reading books or doing research on-line.

Incorporating the customer's perspective is an innovative idea that I developed about twelve years ago. This is why I call my exclusive training technique "Perception Awareness Training." I think we need to look at ourselves and our behaviors from the customer's perspective. I think if we do that, it's going to tell us more about how we should be doing our job. As an example: If you are a banker and Jack is an employee who does not like shaking people's hands because he is paranoid about germs, he may not offer the customer a handshake. Think about what the customer's perception might be in that case. The perception might be, "He is not shaking my hand so is he uncomfortable with me, or is he uncomfortable with himself? Maybe he lacks confidence. So, do I want to do business with someone who is either uncomfortable with me or uncomfortable with himself? I don't think so."

Another situation might be a teller, cashier, retail clerk, or other front-line employee who does not maintain good eye contact with customers. As a leader and coach, you might sit down with that employee and open some dialogue beginning with a statement such as, "If you went to a car lot to buy a used car and the salesperson was not looking you in the eyes, what might your perception be of that salesperson?"

The employee might reply, "He would seem shifty and might be trying to rip me off."

You might ask the employee, "What else?"

The employee might say, "Maybe he doesn't have any confidence in himself and that's why he is not looking me in the eyes."

"Maybe that is true, and maybe it isn't," you say. Then you might ask the employee, "Is that the reality of that salesperson or is that simply your perception of that salesperson?"

"That is just my perception," the employee will probably reply.

I would then ask the question, "Is there any possibility that customers are creating misperceptions about your lack of eye contact as well?"

Some switches should flip on in the employee's brain and you might hear him or her say, "Wow, I never thought about that."

Lastly, we need to make sure we accommodate all three learning styles in our training in order to be effective trainers. Those three styles are visual, auditory, and kinesthetic. It is important to incorporate techniques into our training that accommodate all three learning styles. This means we might provide worksheets, use PowerPoint or flip charts, ask questions to keep them active and involved, use good pitch and tone in our voice, and use frequent humor when teaching. If we try to treat everybody the same, we will fail, which is a tremendous disservice to the people we lead.

All the training I do is customized because there's no such thing as one-size-fits-all. I don't treat all industries or organizations the same because they are not. Training that is not as methodical as I have described can be a waste of an organization's resources and employees' time.

Wright

It's great to hire the right people and train them properly, but how do you monitor them to make sure they are doing what you ask?

Worthley

Well I love the saying, "You cannot manage what you cannot measure." It's important to have measurement tools in place and I believe it's good to have more than one. You should have some type of metrics to keep track of your employees and their productivity (key performance indicators). One of those tools could be mystery shopping (sometimes referred to as secret shopping). Mystery shopping gives you the customer's perspective. Basically, shoppers are sent into your organization (or they telephone in) and they act just like customers. They will provide you with feedback about their experience as a customer and will score it for you.

Genesis Group, one of the companies I owned for about twelve years, was one of the largest mystery shopping companies in the United States during that time. I was also very active in what is called the Mystery Shopping Providers Association. This is an organization of companies that provide mystery shopping services worldwide. In 2000 the Mystery Shopping Providers Association honored me with their Volunteer of the Year award. In 2001 I was awarded the Hall of Fame award. And in 2002 I was elected President of the Mystery Shopping Providers Association. If you are looking for a great provider to help you mystery shop your organization, please feel free to contact me either by telephone or e-mail and I will be glad to recommend some great companies to assist you.

Mystery shopping provides the best level of accountability in terms of modifying behavior because you actually have employees' names, dates, times, and very specific behaviors measured. I believe that is why mystery shopping is one of the better tools for behavior modification because employees know their performance can be measured by any customer coming through the door or calling (and they do not know which one).

If you are looking for a tool to simply measure and monitor customer satisfaction, you can use customer satisfaction surveys. These can be done by mailing surveys to your customers, sending them electronically, or calling them. For best results you should try to send surveys out within a week or so after a customer has done business with you. The longer you wait after a transaction or interaction, the lower the response rate and the less the customer will remember about his or her experience.

You can also use an IVR (Interactive Voice Response) survey, which is inexpensive and it can give you good feedback about your customers' level of satisfaction. The IVR is performed over the telephone and the survey questions are read to the customer by a computer. The questions can normally be answered verbally or by pushing keys on the telephone. The IVR is easy to administer once it is set up because a telephone number and access code can be automatically printed on each customer's receipt. The customer can do the survey from the comfort of his or her home or car with just a telephone. The feedback from customer surveys or an IVR tend to be generalized. They may not be about a specific person or specific action but more about the overall level of customer satisfaction. They can be good for providing metrics and monitoring service levels but may not be as good for changing specific employee behavior.

The challenge about not being able to identify which employee is responsible for bad service is that most employees do not think they are the problem. We do employee surveys for most of our clients and we always ask the employees about the level of service offered by them and their co-workers; the results are always similar. On the average, when you ask employees how they rate the level of service they offer, about 50 percent will say they offer outstanding service. When asked what the level of service they think their co-workers offer, they will say that about 25 percent offer outstanding service. The results consistently show that most employees believe most poor customer service comes from their co-workers and not themselves.

Another method for measuring service quality is called call monitoring, which is used in call centers, service desks, or help desks where the telephone is the primary customer contact. Even though call monitoring is one of the most common tools used to monitor service in these environments, you don't necessarily get the customer's complete perspective because the supervisors who are doing the monitoring are not going through the entire call process. They are not getting the full customer experience so even though they can provide great feedback to employees about their performance on the calls, the customer's perspective may not be complete without going through the entire dial-in, menu, hold, and transfer process. It is also very common for most supervisors to not schedule adequate time for monitoring. Call monitoring can take a lot of time each day and can become monotonous, which is why I think it is not done as often as it needs to be.

Wright

I can see where it's important to measure employee performance to make sure they are doing the things we asked, but how does a company work to help prevent employees from failing in the first place?

Worthley

I am a huge believer that employees don't fail as much as systems do and if leaders would work more proactively to help put great systems in place to help prevent employee failure, the world would be a much better place to live and work. That is simply another huge difference between a "manager" and a "leader." Managers don't normally like change so even though their systems or procedures may not be working well, they are prone to keeping them the same no matter how painful they may be.

If an organization experiences procedure or system failure, leaders should not care who failed because it doesn't make any difference. Instead they should ask, "What are we going to do to make sure this never happens to any of our employees again?" A leader's role is to look ahead and make sure employees have great systems and procedures in place to help make them successful. It's like putting safety nets under employees to help catch them and keep them safe. This is even more critical if you operate a chain store, franchise, or have multiple locations because the consistency of your service and the quality of your process is absolutely critical to a service culture. McDonald's, Subway, or Starbucks would not have grown to be the powerhouses they are today without excellent systems in place to perpetuate consistency and to prevent employees from failing.

Just think about how exposed franchises are to having their brand destroyed by even just one franchise operator if service is poor or the product at that location is defective. Bad publicity can impact all franchise owners worldwide as it did with Jack-in-the-Box years ago when they had some isolated problems with E-coli in the Seattle area, and the more recent E-coli issues with Taco Bell. Even though it was only a problem in a few locations, the ramifications were huge throughout both chains.

Wright

What does a business with a great service culture have that other businesses do not?

Worthley

They live by the mantra, "If you want things that no one else has, you must be willing to do things that no one else is willing to do." I have leaders in organizations tell me that they don't want to serve coffee in the lobby because their carpets might get dirty from spilled coffee. They don't want water coolers in the lobby because children might play with it and get water on the floor. They don't want cookies in the lobby because of cookie crumbs on the floor and some people take too many of them. They don't want popcorn in the lobby because it makes too much of a mess and they have to vacuum it up. They don't want candy dishes in the lobby because people leave their wrappers lying around, which creates a mess. They don't want to stand and greet the customers because it's too tiring on busy days. And they don't want to use a customer's name because some names are too difficult to pronounce.

Organizations spend so much time trying to think about why they can't do things. I wish they would spend more time thinking about what they *can* do, because if exceeding customer expectations or having a service culture was easy, then everybody would be doing it. Creating service cultures is not fast, is not easy, and is not always convenient, but it is done every single day by organizations that are committed to the process and understand that anything less is not an option.

One of my favorite businesses is Les Schwab Tire Centers. They are based in Prineville, Oregon, and have over four hundred locations on the West Coast. Their employees will run out to the parking lot to greet you and then walk you into the showroom. Now, do you think that was a popular decision with their employees when they heard about it? Heck no! They offer fresh popcorn and coffee all day long, and do you think that is convenient for the employees? No! They offer free flat tire repair to everyone, even if you are not a customer. That takes lots of time out of their day and is probably not convenient for their employees. But those are the reasons they dominate the business in almost every town they are in. That is what is required today if you want to stand out from your competition.

The rewards are too great to abandon the journey to a service culture. If what you are doing today is not getting you there, then you need to readjust and go at it again. As you have probably heard, the definition of insanity is to continue to do what you are doing today but expect better results tomorrow. Creating a service culture has so many benefits. You end up with employees who actually love their job and they enjoy where they work. You also have customers who love to do business with you and they tell everybody about you, which also makes them look good as well. A service culture is not just about the external customer, it's about the internal customer as well because employees serve each other in many ways.

Wright

Surely there's a cost to all of this. How can companies be sure they will get the return on their investment?

Worthley

There's been a lot of research done to validate the profit chain that is very clear and easy to quantify. Great Leadership = High Employee Satisfaction = High Customer Satisfaction = High Profits. There have been many businesses that have performed employee satisfaction surveys on each location within their organizations. Then they performed customer satisfaction surveys at each location to see how happy the customers are. Then they evaluated the profitability of each location. We see the same thing over and over again: the locations that have the highest employee satisfaction also have the highest customer satisfaction, and have the highest profitability. But if you go back to the beginning of the profit chain and look at what it takes to have highly satisfied employees, it's great leaders leading them. It's very easy to understand, but so few companies do anything other than give leadership change lip service.

Everything I've talked about today comes down to great leadership. So I'll leave you with my final thought: "The role of a great leader is to leave a footprint of success and not a path of destruction."

Wright

Today we've been talking with Brad Worthley. He is internationally acclaimed as a leadership and customer service expert who has trained hundreds of thousands of people in a wide range of industries throughout the world. He teaches businesses how to consistently build and train both customer and employee loyalty by changing their culture and not just their people.

Brad, thank you so much for being with us today on *Speaking of Success.*

Worthley

My pleasure.

About the Author

BRAD WORTHLEY is the founder and CEO of Brad Worthley International, Inc., a Bellevue, Washington, based consulting and training firm. Brad, an accomplished consultant with over thirty-two years of business management experience, is also an internationally acclaimed leadership and customer service expert. He has trained hundreds of thousands of people throughout a wide range of industries. A true professional, Brad equips companies with dynamic customer service and leadership essentials. He teaches leading corporations how to consistently build and retain customer loyalty using his proven methods.

Brad is also the creator of a revolutionary new concept in modifying behavior called "Perception Awareness Training," This method keeps seminar participants entertained while helping them retain the information they learn. He is a master storyteller and delivers his powerful message from the customer's perspective with sincerity and humor. Many have referred to his lively presentations as "shows." Brad is always one of the highest rated speakers at any event where he speaks.

After college and an associate of science degree, Brad started his business career at the age of twenty by opening his first successful business—a sporting goods store. Since then, Brad has created and sold six other very successful businesses in the fields of retail, wholesale, marketing, distribution, and consulting. He has experienced every aspect of the business world, and not only talks the talk, but walks the walk.

Brad is past President of the Mystery Shopping Providers Association in 2002–2003. The organization's goal is dedicated to improving customer service. Brad was awarded its "Volunteer of the Year Award" for 2001, and was awarded the highest honor in the industry in 2002—the "Hall of Fame Award."

Brad Worthley International, Inc.
12819 SE 38th St. #375
Bellevue, WA 98006
Phone: 425.957-9696
E-mail: Brad@BradWorthley.com
www.BradWorthley.com

Chapter 13

DR. JAN NORTHUP

David Wright (Wright)

Today we are speaking with Dr. Jan Northup. She is president of Management Training Systems, Inc. She is an internationally known author, speaker, organizational strategist, training specialist, and business coach. For the past twenty-five years, Jan has focused her efforts on working with senior leaders in both public and private organizations in the areas of organizational effectiveness and employee performance management.

Through strategic planning facilitation, developing employee recruitment and retention processes, establishing employee mentoring programs and conducting team building, conflict resolution and communications training for employees, Jan has led organizations as they embraced change and moved to higher levels of innovation and tangible results.

Dr. Northup, welcome to *Speaking of Success.*

Dr. Jan Northup (Northup)

Thank you, Mr. Wright.

Wright

Let's start with your topic, "The Promotable Woman: Have We Come a Long Way Baby?" Have women really come a long way?

Northup

You would think that the issues women face in the workplace today would be settled. It's not exactly the dawning of the women's movement, nor is it the first time anyone has addressed what it takes for women to be successful. Women have come a long way. And we have a long way to go to gain equality as professionals in the workplace as well as in our paychecks.

Wright

What has changed or hasn't changed since your first research project?

Northup

Twenty years after I first researched and published on the topic of the promotable woman, I find that women are still trying to overcome some stereotypes about their skills and capabilities and their commitment to their career. They are searching for ways to excel professionally while meeting the traditional demands of wife, partner, mother, daughter, sister, friend, community member, and caregiver. There are still a lot of assumptions by many that women are working only to bring in extra money, a second income, or just to help out with family expenses, when in reality, many women in the workplace today are also the heads of their household.

Wright

Let's go back to the title—who is a "promotable woman"? Can women achieve success in non-traditional jobs or what some still consider a male-dominated workplace?

Northup

Let's address the first part of the question. What is a promotable woman? A promotable woman is a woman who is recognized for her achievements. She role models the success factors associated with being considered productive, professional, and confident in her job or in her career. Being promotable is not necessarily going for a higher-level job, but rather promoting the idea that she is competent and capable of taking on higher levels of responsibility. She may, in fact, want to stay in the job she has but she wants to be seen as a professional and wants the opportunity to continue to improve her skills or to take on more meaningful projects.

To address the second part of your question, more and more women are holding significant jobs in non-traditional fields—those roles previously held by men. In past generations, men did not expect to see women in the workplace but rather at home caring for the children, managing the household, and being a support system to their husbands. It was not considered proper for a woman to work outside the home or, if she did, it was in a support role such as a secretary or receptionist within a company or organization. She might also work as a nurse, teacher, librarian, waitress, maid, cashier, or stewardess, to name a few. Another perception was that the money she earned was used as a second income and that there was a male member of the household providing the primary financial support. We shouldn't forget those women who were supporting themselves and their families—single women as heads of the household were not recognized.

As times changed, women began focusing on gaining more skills, education, and training and they entered colleges, technical schools, and businesses with the goal of performing jobs with equal skills and for equal pay. Sitting side-by-side with male classmates, the image of what women could contribute began changing. Generational expectations changed. Men were accustomed to seeing women in the classroom so it was not a big jump to see them in the workplace. With divorce, remarriage, or not getting married at all, the structure of families also changed and left more women as head of their households. Prior to attention given to child support and spousal support initiatives, women were often raising their children with no outside financial support. So working was not just something to do in their spare time or to bring in extra income but for survival and providing a quality of life for their families. To do that a woman needed to integrate the seven success factors women have told us are critical if they are to achieve success.

Wright

So what are the success factors?

Northup

From my research, seven primary factors were identified by almost every woman we surveyed. Our survey respondents included women from entry level positions to presidential appointees and women from traditional and non-traditional career fields. In addition to surveying women, men were surveyed and asked what factors were critical for their success. While most success factors are important for both men and women, regardless of gender, women reported specific needs that men did not report as being critical.

The first success factor is *Prosperity Thinking*. Prosperity Thinking is believing that there is an abundance of opportunities available for you. It's creating a vision of where you want to be in your personal and professional life and then developing and using the *Posture of Excellence* as one tool to move you toward your goals.

Wright

The Posture of Excellence? Do you mean standing up straight with a book on your head?

Northup

In a way it does have to do with physical posture. But before we can stand up straight on the outside, we have to stand tall on the inside. We talk to ourselves at about eight hundred to one thousand words a minute all day long. We talk to ourselves in supporting or positive language or we degrade ourselves by talking negatively about who we are, how we are doing our job, or how we are going to have conversations with others.

Let me give you some examples. You're just given an assignment or a project. Your first reaction or self-talk might be, "How will I ever find time to get this done?" *or* "I always get the crummy assignments," *or* "I've never done anything like this before." If this is the case, you are in a defeatist posture. This is the time to use the Posture of Excellence.

The Posture of Excellence is recognizing when you are limiting yourself with any negative thoughts, pulling yourself out of those negative thoughts by remembering past positive events, and turning those negative or limiting thoughts into a positive attitude and positive self-talk about what you *can* do.

In the future when you are given a new assignment, here are some examples of positive self-talk: "I love challenging assignments" or, "What a great opportunity to work with a new project (team)" or, "This is a chance for me to show what I know and can do" or, "Bring it on!"

The Posture of Excellence is one of the most powerful tools for moving forward in a positive direction.

Wright

Your second success factor is *Patterns for Power.* So you teach women to put on their boxing gloves?

Northup

Sometimes we have to put on the imaginary boxing gloves, but basically it doesn't mean power over someone else or a power struggle with someone else, but rather understanding and tapping into the power that communication plays in working with others and our own ability to communicate our talents and capabilities. It's also being able to negotiate what you want through your communication skills; it's understanding your own style of communicating, understanding the communication styles of others, and then working with those people in a way that produces outcomes that you desire.

Communication skills can make or break a career. We know that people are hired for their technical skills, their experience, or their expertise, but are reassigned, demoted, or even fired for their lack of interpersonal skills. Plainly put, no one wants to work with someone who is negative or difficult. Powerful communication skills put you in control of daily interactions and eventually your work and your life.

Wright

Do you think that women can do it all? We hear a lot of things. We go to all kinds of programs about how to balance home and career. Do you really think that women can have a successful career and meet their family and home obligations at the same time?

Northup

As a friend of mine told me, "You can do it all, just not at the same time." Women try to do too much and end up trying to manage what we call a three ring circus: taking care of their career in one ring, taking care of their family in another, and taking care of all other obligations in the third ring. What's often overlooked is taking care of themselves. Many women have told me that they only feel truly successful when they have a sense of control and balance between their multiple roles and responsibilities.

So how do you achieve this balance? That leads us to the third success factor: *Positioning.* We need to *position* ourselves with an environment for success and with skills and people who will bring out the best in us. This will help us create that balance. It's knowing when and how to handle the multiple and at times competing roles and responsibilities. As a professional, a caregiver, a companion, a family member, a volunteer, we need to be aware of the roles that we take on every day. Balancing home and career is one factor that men rarely mentioned in our surveys as being critical to their success.

Studies report that one of the most important factors for women in creating balance between their career and their personal life is to have the wholehearted support of a spouse or significant other. They need to have more energy givers than energy robbers. What that really means is first you need those people around you who will help you with your tasks or just be a sounding board and provide a safe environment when you work through the balancing act. Included in your *personal support system* might be a counselor or a therapist as well as those who can offer you some specific direction or strategies for dealing with competing demands that you might have.

And then, in addition to a personal support system, you need to have a *professional support system*. A professional support system includes mentors, coaches, advisors, peers, or anyone else who can help you as you grow within your job or your profession. We also found women reporting the greatest achievements and the quickest levels of success when they had professional mentors or professional coaches.

A mentor or a coach can offer you the wisdom of his or her experience. Coaches can challenge you to look at your goals or they can propel you into action. In addition, mentors or coaches can offer you encouragement along the way. They may give you that swift kick that pulls you out of your comfort zone and helps you identify new opportunities. Possibilities now become realities.

It is interesting to note that another difference between men and women in their responses is related to having mentors. Men reported being assigned a mentor either formally or informally when they began a new job or as they progressed within their organization. They were taught about the financial operations, the politics, the unspoken rules for getting ahead, and the dues they would have to pay to be seen as a team player. Women reported that someone usually taught them a specific job but when it came to learning about organizational issues and opportunities, they rarely had been assigned a mentor. Most who reported advancing in their careers said that they had to seek out mentors on their own.

Other professionals who might help you along the way may be your peers, people who have been in the same type of job, or people who have faced similar situations. They can offer you advice on the steps they took to get where they needed to be.

I also want to talk about the *skills* that are necessary for success. The first skill that was mentioned over and over was being able to *speak well* in front of other people. The second skill was being able to *write well* and the third skill was *trusting your intuition.*

It is assumed that people who write and speak well are more knowledgeable than those who cannot write or speak well. We can think of examples where people we knew were experts on specific subjects. They stepped to the front of the room and did not present well orally. Another person who may not have been as competent or had as many skills or had as good a background, but who was a fluent speaker, was perceived as knowing more. Whether presenting to a small group of people or to an audience of hundreds, men and women need to hone their speaking skills as a way of demonstrating their capabilities and competence.

The same applies to writing skills, especially in light of the number of written communications that are made through e-mails. We need to take a look at how we write and to know when we can write in abbreviated messages or when we need to spend more time composing and outlining in a logical way what we are trying to communicate.

The third skill, trusting your intuition, is often called a gut-level reaction in men and intuition in women. No matter what we call it, women need to be aware of their sixth sense or the ability to know what feels right or congruent and what feels incongruent in their life. Then they can focus on maintaining those things that are congruent and decide what to do about incongruencies.

Wright

So how do we manage stress in such a fast-paced society?

Northup

I'm glad you asked that. We live in such a fast-paced society of competing demands, regardless of gender. Staying with the theme of Prosperity Thinking, the first success factor, I'd like to approach it from the standpoint of looking at what provides comfort in your life. So that's the fourth success factor—*Prescriptions for Comfort Management.*

If you've ever been asked to go to a stress management seminar, you probably became stressed thinking about the fact that you are going to talk about what stresses you. So what we want to do is talk about what we need in our physical environment and what we need in our people environment that gives us the most comfort. We know that when we are in our comfort zone we think more clearly, we make better decisions, and demonstrate our capabilities and skills in a more positive way than when we are stressed. We also know that when we are in our comfort zone, as opposed to being stressed, we take more time to think about the way that we word our communications. Do you see how the success factors all build upon each other?

So while we are in our comfort zone we can really focus on having optimal performance levels in each one of the success factors. The first step in controlling stress is to identify what stresses you. What situations, what events, what people seem to cause you discomfort or a feeling that you are at a breaking point or not in control? When people were asked to define what stress meant to them, they often said that it was when they felt out of control. So we want to get people in a place of comfort where they are feeling in control of the situation and then practice stress management techniques when they find that they are under stress.

Not every technique works for everyone. Each person has to decide what technique is most compatible with their lifestyle. Some of the basic techniques that we suggest, and one of the simplest, is physical exercise. That can range from working out, dancing, playing sports, running a marathon, or simply walking during a lunch break or before or after work. A second technique is practicing relaxation exercises. This could be yoga, meditation, or simply sitting and listening to soft music. It could be finding a quiet place to get away from the noise of any particular situation and just think through what's happening to you, what's happening to others, and particularly finding outlets that will keep distracting negative self-talk from taking control. When you are stressed, you can simply delve into a hobby or a passion that you have, a volunteer activity, a community event— something to take your thoughts away from that stressful situation. We need to learn to play.

Wright

You mention play as a success factor. Who has time to play?

Northup

That's a good question. As adults we have forgotten the therapeutic value of play. We think that we are too busy to take time to play but incorporating the fifth success factor, *Programming for Play,* is important. We need to find people with whom we are totally comfortable and with whom we can enjoy ourselves without fear of being judged or being concerned that people will think we are not taking life seriously.

Play contributes to overall good health. Even when we think we are too busy, it is important that we make it a priority to take time to take a deep breath, take a break from the routine, and find more ways to put fun and laughter in our lives.

When we are playing, we are reenergizing. When we are reenergized, we have time to clear out the cobwebs and make room for creative and innovative ideas. It is like adding fuel to our car's gas tank—play keeps us running.

Wright

In your book you quote Joe Louis, the boxer, who said, "I've been rich and I've been poor. And rich is better!" Are you trying to say only the rich are successful?

Northup

Not at all. It would be nice if we were all Donald Trumps. That would be fantastic. But the point to be considered when we talk about the sixth success factor, *Principle and Interest,* is to understand the role finance and money play in our life and our success. The first step is to understand that money provides a resource necessary for our lifetime development. Investing in a professional resume writer or interviewing skills coach might give the needed edge if applying for a job. We may invest in additional education and training, invest in starting a new business, or invest in a new product, a new service, or a new innovation in a current business. We may want to invest in an image consultant. An image consultant may offer strategies for improving physical appearance or may serve as a voice or writing coach.

Another important step in Principle and Interest is to understand the financial inner-workings of your organization. Women have not always been actively involved in the financial side of their organization, which is one of the requirements that men reported in our surveys. What I mean by financial inner-workings is understanding the financial trends of the organization. When are things going great? When are the budgets ample? When are there new monies being put into certain areas of the company, certain projects or new product or service development?

Women need to look for opportunities where they might be able to move into specific projects or divisions that are experiencing growth. Conversely, women need to be aware of budget cuts. Perhaps a product line is being eliminated or sales have not been as great during a particular quarter so budgets may have to be realigned. That should offer insight on whether that particular budget compromise will affect a project on which they are working on or even affect their job.

Wright

Your final success factor is having a purpose. Why is this unique? Don't most of us have a purpose?

Northup

We all do have a purpose whether that is about maintaining where we are or changing where we are to something different. The final success factor, *Purposing,* is where we roll up our sleeves and put effort into that purpose. Purpose moves from a noun (a thing) to a verb (an action).

In interviewing both men and women, we asked them to share their goals and vision of their future in both their personal lives and their professional lives. Many could easily relate their goals to us while others said they either didn't have goals or their answers didn't seem to have clearly defined goals.

We also found that as we asked them to share their vision or their goals, their wants, and their desires with us, many women told us what they *didn't* want in their future. Almost without exception, men told us what they *did* want.

When thinking about their future, men saw abundance and practiced Prosperity Thinking. They focused on what they were moving *toward* instead of what they were moving away *from.* Going back to Prosperity Thinking, a critical element to success for women is the need to focus on where they want to go, not away from what they don't want.

Most of us do have goals whether we consciously think about them every day, think about them occasionally, or subconsciously move toward a certain outcome. Here are two of my favorite quotes about the need for Purposing:

> "If you don't know where you are going,
> any road will get you there."

"If you don't know where you are going,
you might end up somewhere else."

So if we, in fact, want to have a secure future and have the outcomes of our efforts produce what we have envisioned for ourselves, we need to have clear goals *and* we need to write down those goals. We also need to visualize and repeat our goals aloud *every day.* Goals should be phrased in a positive way (what we want) so we are concentrating and moving toward the future that we know is available to us and that will bring a sense of satisfaction and fulfillment.

To reinforce that we can achieve what we want, we need to focus on our past successes. We don't want to focus on failure because that only counteracts a Posture of Excellence and short-circuits the energy we need to take positive action.

The bottom line is that remembering and focusing on past successes reenergizes us and gives us the confidence that we can have success again in the future.

Okay, so we have our goals in mind. Now what? We need to take actions that will get us to our goals. We need to write down our goals, read them every day, and visualize (see in our mind) the successful outcome or the end result we want. Remember—goals should be written positively and focus on what we want not what we don't want.

Wright
What final advice will you give to women who want to find success?

Northup
I think the first and most important piece of advice for anyone would be: don't get in your own way. Believe that success is possible for you and then think one positive thought and take one specific action every single day that moves you closer to your goals. *Remember that yard by yard it's hard, but inch by inch it's a cinch.*

Secondly, don't be concerned about what others think about your desire to be successful. You need only to answer to yourself. Hold the image that you are a Promotable Woman and form alliances—regardless of gender. Find strong women *and* strong men who can help you develop strategies that will lead to your success.

Finally, I would challenge every woman to answer the question, "How can I meet the demands of building a successful career and meeting my personal obligations?" Remember that you *can* do it all, just not at the same time. You may need to make trade-offs, prioritize activities, develop time management skills, and build your personal and professional support systems.

Wright

What a great conversation. I've learned a lot today. I want to thank you for participating in this project.

Today we've been talking with Dr. Jan Northup. She has created "The Promotable Woman: What Makes the Difference" video training program that was featured on the Public Broadcasting Service. Close to a million people worldwide have attended her seminars, training classes, and presentations. She has been the featured speaker at numerous regional and national conferences and was the first woman to conduct a nationwide speaking tour of Australia on women's management issues. Dr. Northup's latest book is *Life's a Bitch And Then You Change Your Attitude: 5 Secrets to Taming Life's Roller Coaster and Building Resilience,* which examines personal and organizational resilience (I can't wait to read that one).

Dr. Northup, thank you so much for being with us today on *Speaking of Success.*

Northup

Thank you, Mr. Wright.

About the Author

DR. JAN NORTHUP is an internationally known author, speaker, organizational strategist, and training specialist. With a degree in education, she has almost thirty years experience in teaching and training development. For the past twenty-five years, Jan has focused her efforts on working with public and private organizations in the areas of employee performance management. As a Professional Behavioral and Values Analyst, she has assisted organizations in meeting all aspects of talent management and employee development through customized training programs and individual and group coaching.

At the same time, she has kept her ties with academia by developing and teaching undergraduate and graduate courses in the areas of organizational design, team building, leadership, and marketing. An on-line course developer, instructor, and adjunct faculty member at Bellevue University, Jan has taught at numerous universities including Thunderbird, The American Graduate School of International Management, and George Washington University.

Advanced training in non-confrontational verbal skills facilitation was such an invaluable tool in working with group dynamics and problem-solving that it led Dr. Northup to develop the S.P.A.C.E. (Superior Performance and Communications Excellence) training program which has been given in private and government environments.

Dr. Northup created "The Promotable Woman: What Makes the Difference" video training program that has been featured on the Public Broadcasting Service. She has made frequent radio and television appearances, discussing the factors that make the difference in the lives of successful people. Close to a million people worldwide have attended her seminars, training classes, and presentations. She has been a featured speaker at numerous regional and national conferences and was the first woman to conduct a nationwide speaking tour of Australia on women's management issues. In recognition of her professional and community accomplishments, she has been the recipient of numerous awards and commendations. She is a member of the Phoenix Chamber of Commerce facilitating the Professional Women's Roundtable, a life-time member of the American Association of University Women, and has served on the Board of Directors for Girls Ranch Inc. of Arizona. Dr. Northup's latest book, *Life's a Bitch and Then You Change Your Attitude: 5 Secrets to Taming Life's Roller Coaster and Building Resilience,* examines personal and organizational resilience.

Dr. Jan Northup
Management Training Systems, Inc.
P.O. Box 11806
Glendale, AZ 85318
Phone: 623.587.7644
E-mail: jnkmts@msn.com
www.trainingperformance.com
www.thebizcoach4u.com

Chapter 14

BRANDON IURATO

David Wright (Wright)
Today we're talking with Brandon Iurato. He is Founder and President of Success Strategies, a training and development company that focuses on maximizing human potential.

Since 2000, Brandon has experienced a meteoric rise as a professional speaker, trainer, and consultant in both professional and personal performance. Even having no formal experience or education, he has gone straight to the top. Uncommon commitment in the area of passion and enthusiasm, an unwavering positive mental attitude, and a sincere desire to help others has facilitated his success.

Brandon is a professional member of the National Speakers Association, American Society of Training and Development, and Toastmasters International, a communication and leadership development organization.

Brandon, welcome to *Speaking of Success.*

Brandon Iurato (Iurato)
Thank you very much, David, it's good to be here.

Wright

You seem to be a strong believer in passion and enthusiasm as related to success. Would you tell our readers why?

Iurato

Let me start by quoting Dale Carnegie, this is a great opener. He said, "Flaming enthusiasm backed up by horse sense and persistence is a quality that most frequently makes for success." You know, at times I wonder if people realize the meaning and importance of enthusiasm. Enthusiasm comes from the Greek word *en-theos*, meaning "the God within." And enthusiasm is the outward manifestation of inner-passion—it's our spirit. Passion and enthusiasm go hand-in-hand. One cannot exist without the other. I find that when you are passionate about something—whether it is a career, a hobby, a relationship, a cause—pure enthusiasm will manifest itself naturally.

French philosopher, Dennis Diderot, said, "Only passions, great passions, can elevate the soul to great things." I love that. For many people—we pass them by every day—there isn't a twinkle in their eye, only emptiness it seems, and lost hope. They say you can live about thirty days without food, three days without water, but only one second without hope. However, with hope, you dream, you think, you work, and with hope you foster enthusiasm. I tell folks to think of a time when there was a passion inside them—a driving force—that made them feel good, empowered, and spirited. Enthusiasm can often carry us far beyond any skill or talent we may have. Arthur James Balfour, former British Prime Minister, said it best: "Enthusiasm moves the world."

Wright

Why do you think failure is so popular or so common?

Iurato

Over the years I thought this was a trick question. Let me explain. When something negative or bad happens to people, they automatically turn on themselves through a negative subconscious programming and they perceive themselves as failures. This is odd behavior because I think failure is something that happens *to* you. It is an event, not a person. And part of this problem is how failure and fear feed off each other. Nothing collapses our horizons or poisons the present like fear. We fear many things: death, disease, failure, poverty, pain, humiliation, stupidity, rejection and that's just for starters.

Fear can act like a cattle chute, keeping us in line and moving us in the direction that we have given up control over. We end up on auto-pilot, heading down the road of failure and mediocrity.

Even though there are countless things to be scared of, and there are more and more being added to the list every day, they all have one thing in common: each and every one of them is a creation of our own minds. They've been put there over the years by our own thinking, our behaviors, our subconscious. They say one of the greatest jokes in psychology is this: When we finally have the courage to journey into the center of our fears, you know what we find? Nothing. Nothing except the layers and layers of fears we put there. They are the fears that control and manipulate us to do nothing, be the same, never risk, and stay within the confines of our comfort zone. Now without us to give them light and feed them, the things we fear are like Halloween masks—they are fearsome on the surface but devoid of any power. Once we accept the surface appearances as real, life is breathed into them. It's not a kind and gentle life either. No, it is like bringing a ferocious pit bull to life and training it to attack yourself.

Throughout our lives, giving in to our fears happens quite often. We soon expect failure and mediocrity to be part of our lives. I believe a key component here is learning to train ourselves and to reprogram our subconscious thoughts. Now, don't get me wrong here; it's easier said than done. Our subconscious is very powerful and unrelenting. To put positive thoughts into our brain and to take positive action requires commitment and effort. Do you see the pattern here?

Wright

Absolutely. What do you believe are the common obstacles to achieving this success?

Iurato

There are many. And they reveal themselves anytime, anywhere. Often, we summon them up on our own. How? I believe the most powerful reason is a true lack of belief and faith in ourselves and our ability. When we lack belief and hope, we remain a slave to our comfort zones. We are essentially trapped. When we are stuck in our comfort zone, no one can reach us and we can't reach out to others. Nothing happens, there's no growth, and nothing new and daring is being attempted.

Our comfort zone commands us to stay where we are—in that same boring job for over twenty years, in that same abusive, emotionally draining, and damaging relationship. In order to raise our self-esteem and gain the necessary confidence in attempting a difficult task, we have to stretch and expand our comfort zone. View your comfort zone as if it were a rubber-band; it only works when it's stretched or expanded. I remained in my safe comfort zone for twenty-five years. My life changed *completely* when I stopped listening to that voice—that little voice that said, "Don't try it, you'll fail."

There are many things I had to do that I really didn't want to do. They were difficult, time consuming, some even required a financial investment, and most I was just plain afraid to do. But I had to do them in order to get what I wanted—my dreams.

We are all sitting on tons of untapped potential and we don't even know it. This fact alone causes the many underlying obstacles to surface—lack of goals, poor planning, procrastination, negativity, time wasters, waiting for the right moment, and so on. People seem to give up too quickly.

When people truly believe they are capable of wonderful things and they develop the necessary passion and enthusiasm and go after it, *nothing* can stop them.

When I think of failure, Abraham Lincoln comes to mind. This man was the epitome and spirit of perseverance. He failed miserably at business and politics for thirty-five years before becoming our sixteenth President of the United States.

I go by H. Jackson Brown's Two Rules of Perseverance: "Rule number one: take one more step. Rule number two: when you don't think you can take one more step, refer to rule number one."

Wright

You speak about "WhyPower" saying that this must be our driving force, what do you mean by this?

Iurato

Well, "WhyPower"—it sounds powerful in itself, doesn't it? Why-power is simply the unstoppable strength and energy created from the discovery and understanding of your purpose in life and career. It sounds simple and easy, but it is critical in building our foundation for moving forward. For us to become focused, driven individuals wanting to move forward and getting closer to our dreams and goals, we must stay connected to our definite major purpose. That might be our reason for getting up in the morning. Is it to go to work to pay the bills or is it to secure a stable future for you and your family? Is it just to get by and live paycheck to paycheck or is it to leave a legacy? You choose, but it had better be big. It must be worthy—have meaning. It must be critically important to you or when things get tough, the easy thing to do is quit. Unfortunately, this is what happens to many people over the years, day in and day out.

When there's a *reason* to grab life and do something, there will be a way to do it. Nietzsche put it this way, for a person who has a why to live for, that person can bear almost any how. The why is the tough part—it is 90 percent of the success equation—the how is only 10 percent. I can teach people *how* to be successful; I can teach a group of people how to succeed in sales; I can teach people how to build a model airplane, but I can't teach them *why*.

Wright

Oddly enough, you come from a law enforcement background; how did you migrate to motivational speaking?

Iurato

I spent a total of thirteen years in military and federal law enforcement. I left my law enforcement career in 2000, which wasn't that long ago. It was a difficult decision for me—fighting crime was meant to be my career. About six years into my police career, attitudes and negativity surrounding my job seemed to be getting out of control and it was affecting my own attitude and demeanor. I would go home in a bad mood and wake up in an even worse mood! At times, I didn't even want to go into work.

To escape this downward spiral that I saw happening, I began to read again. I read non-fiction, motivation, and self-help books, just like this one. Things started to change. I looked at things differently. I put together a few workshops with a speaker's bureau I had joined and delivered them during lunchtime. I found that I was helping people. They were laughing and asking for other tips and advice. Word spread quickly; they wanted to attend more seminars. It was a blast! Whether there were five or forty-five participants, it didn't matter—it was fun!

And around the same time, I joined Toastmasters International, a public speaking organization. As my public speaking skills developed, I began to think, "How do I become a professional speaker and trainer? How can I make a living and a life speaking professionally *and* helping others at the same time?"

So I thought that the best way for me to get experience and stage time in front of people would be in the world of corporate training. But I didn't know any corporate trainers, I didn't know anything about corporate training, I didn't have the education, I didn't have the background, I didn't have the experience. I looked past my limitations, put my resume together, and put it on the Web. Within a few weeks, a Fortune 200 company called me in for an interview. When it was all said and done, they hired me as their corporate sales trainer! Keep in mind, no experience, limited education, and no industry knowledge. I wondered, why me?

A few months after I was hired, I asked the Vice-President of sales why he hired me. He said two words: "passion and enthusiasm." I stayed in corporate America for over three years before going out on my own and officially launching my company, Success Strategies, which I founded in 1997.

Wright

Will you tell our readers what drives you to be successful?

Iurato

Several years ago I came across an article about the late actor, Michael Landon. He had success with *Bonanza, Little House on the Prairie,* and *Highway to Heaven.* Sadly, he died in 1991 at the age of fifty-four, from pancreatic cancer. He lived only three months after his diagnosis. Reflecting back on his life, he said that when we are little kids someone should pull us aside and tell us that we are dying every day, then maybe we'll go out there and do something with our lives. You know, I think about that and I take it a step further—what if we were born with an expiration date stamped across our foreheads? Going through life, we would see it every day in the mirror brushing our teeth. Each morning we would be reminded that our days are counting down. Imagine knowing when you are going to die!

It's a safe bet that you'd be out there making something happen. You're not going to go back to bed, ho-hum, thinking you're depressed and pull the covers over your head. No way! Only three years left! Let's go out and *do something* today! The truth is, we all have that expiration date. We just can't see it. Now, knowing this, I'm internally motivated to make things happen in my own life. The sun may not always rise in our world, although we go through life thinking otherwise.

Wright

There are countless books on success, what do you think makes your perspective different?

Iurato

Are you ready for a real pop cliché? *Been there done that.* From my experience, many of the self-help, motivation, and success books (and I've read dozens of them) that are put out are put out by "ivory tower" theorists. They espouse wonderful concepts and ideas but they haven't applied them or put them to test themselves. They aren't living their dreams, but they want to show *you* how to.

I've wasted years of my life searching for the secret to success and never found it. What I did find, however, was if I did certain things in a certain way and changed my behavior, good things happened. I literally had to reprogram myself for success because over the years I had subconsciously conditioned myself for failure. The success strategies that I suggest are point-blank common sense ideas that will change your life if you apply them.

Wright

You speak of EQ being more important than IQ when striving for success. Would you tell our readers what you mean by that?

Iurato

EQ, or emotional intelligence, is a person's ability to interact, act, and react affectively with other people. It's also your own self perception. How you see yourself and how you believe others see you. It goes back over 2000 years ago to Socrates when he advised, "know thyself." Heightened interpersonal skills—the soft skills—will take you much further in life and in today's ever competitive business environment than a 140 IQ.

A friend of mine is a technology genius—he even has a few patents and has held "C" level positions in different companies. But he wonders why he has been with several companies and has had trouble finding work. The truth is, he has poorly developed social and interpersonal skills.

Competition is tough, more and more so today. Your ability to affectively articulate your thoughts and ideas in a clear manner, get along with others in a workplace, and to communicate with peers, subordinates, and upper management will be your key to success. No one really cares how smart you are—that is really what it comes down to. People are more interested in how you can help them solve problems, create possibility, and take their pain away. I can't tell you how many times I've heard a manager say, "Hey, Bob's brilliant but he can't get along with others; no one wants to work with him." Bob will hit a certain level in a corporate hierarchy and stay there. In my business, I have found when people are more aware of who they are, how they interact with others, how well they listen, and truly care about other people in the organization, they'll go a lot further.

Wright

Were you always successful at everything you attempted both personally and professionally?

Iurato

Oh no. I failed at *everything*. Growing up I couldn't do anything right. I was left back in the first grade, I was a mediocre student, I failed high school math, I held numerous jobs, and was fired from many of them. The failure list goes on and on. In the area of athletic competition, whether it was karate, boxing, wrestling, power lifting, I failed many times before ever placing first.

Being a failure allowed me to look at things from a different angle. Failing enabled me to reevaluate a current plan to make adjustments and try again. If it weren't for failing, I wouldn't have the knowledge or life experience that I have today. I learned to invite failure into my world. I envision failure as small stepping stones to my ultimate goal. With the right mindset, failing at something will not faze you. You won't beat yourself up and become negative or discouraged—you simply move forward. Success is imminent.

Wright

What motivates or inspires you?

Iurato

There is just so much to do. There is much to see and experience with such little time. I am very fortunate to have a wife and a business plan that allows me to have about twenty weeks of time off a year to accomplish things in life that are important to me and my family. Knowing that I have a limited time on this planet with family and friends, I need to get going! In my area of expertise, I help others discover their true potential and offer strategies and ideas so they can get more out of life.

The reason helping others is so important to me is because I was once a lost soul—a wandering generality. I was trying to go from point A to point B without a map or a plan. I didn't have a mentor, I didn't have a parent who kicked me in the tail and said, "You are going the wrong way, go this way." I didn't have that teacher in school who said I needed to get on track. I was *off* track for several years, not knowing what to do. Through trial and error, pain and worry, desperation and frustration, *I* discovered the keys to success. I decided that this was much too valuable not to share with others who are in need of encouragement and a better life.

Wright

I have to ask you the great classic: would you define success?

Iurato

I define success by living a life of contentment and meaning, accomplishing tasks and goals you set for yourself that allow you to create the life you were meant to live. When I am able to check off a goal I set for myself that gets me closer to my ultimate destiny, I consider myself successful. It may be to drink eight glasses of water a day; if I accomplish that, I'm successful. Not only do I feel better but I feel better about myself. This feeling brings on a sense of happiness, fulfillment, and motivation.

Now, keep in mind that happiness is a state of mind. I am happy because I think I am. Money and worldly possessions will not bring success or happiness. In my training sessions, when I ask, "What do you want out of life," countless individuals from various backgrounds reply with the two most popular answers: success and/or happiness. Everyone seems to want or strive toward success and happiness. However, I find that people's meaning of success isn't well defined so it eludes them. It is a common misconception that success will bring happiness. A healthy state of mind brings happiness. You need to seek out the things that contribute to your "well being." When this happens, things begin to fall into place.

Wright

What do you think makes you an expert on this subject?

Iurato

A solid, proven track record of failure! Not many "experts" will admit that. Years of failing at everything I did brought me that much closer to success. The choices I made in the past were not connected to the results I wanted to create. So my actions were in direct conflict with my intentions. In the end, I was left with what I settled and compromised for, which wasn't much at all.

After years of failing, I was burned out being mediocre. I started to pay careful attention to what I was really asking of myself; I began to write down all I wanted out of life. Then, I focused on what I call "high pay off" activities. These were the tasks and actions I needed to accomplish to make things happen and eventually get me closer to my goals.

Now I make choices that are linked to the results that I want to create. I envision the end result first, and then plan out the necessary steps to make it come to fruition. Once I started doing this, things started to happen for me. It's been nearly ten years since starting my self-development company and four years being a full-time entrepreneur.

My passion lies in sharing my experience, knowledge, and success strategies with other like-minded individuals. Over the years I've invested tens of thousands of dollars and countless hours in myself to one day be in a position to transfer this knowledge to others. Shared knowledge is power.

The late comedian, Eddie Cantor said, "Overnight success takes about twenty years." I'm getting close. I show people how to shorten the success curve. It doesn't have to take a lifetime. You don't have to wander aimlessly, going from point A to point B without a map or plan wasting several years hoping to find the secret path. Sharing my failure stories and success strategies allows others to see a clearer, more defined path to their destiny.

Wright

You were invited to participate in this book along with other speakers, trainer consultants, and celebrities. We know why we are writing the book, why did you decide to participate?

Iurato

I think the answer lies in the word "hope." I came across an inspirational acronym for the word "H-O-P-E:" *Hang On, Possibilities Exist.* I believe that we all possess incredible talent; at times it just needs to be revealed. Perhaps we will be inspired by a book, a teacher, a friend, a movie, a news story, or an event. Whatever it is, we have the power to cause lasting and positive change in our lives . . . and in the lives of others.

In life we witness many individuals who have a dream and a purpose but somehow their dream and purpose both quickly fade. We are sitting on talent we don't even realize we have. Some of us need a push to reveal our hidden talent so we can achieve greatness within ourselves. The reason I chose to be a part of this book is because there are people out there who don't know where to turn. Hopefully, people will pull this book off the shelf, connect with my story and with those of other authors, and be inspired! By believing in ourselves and in our abilities, and discovering our *why,* we can do great things.

Wright

What are you hoping to deliver to your audience?

Iurato

I like to see people begin to develop a profound sense of direction and possibility in their lives. I want them to know, through effort and commitment they can create wonderful results. When I begin to lose focus and lack direction, I think of a powerful story about an eight-year-old boy who approached an old man by a wishing well. This little boy looked up to the old man's eyes and he said, "I was told you're a very wise man. Can you tell me the secret of life?"

The old man looked down at the youngster and said, "I've thought a lot in my lifetime and the secret can be summed up in four words. The first is *think*—think about the values you wish to live your life by. The second is *believe*—believe in yourself based on the thinking you've done and about the values you are going to live your life by. The third is *dream*—dream about the things that *can* be based on your belief in yourself and the values you are going to live by. And the last is *dare*—dare to make your dreams become a reality based upon belief in yourself and your values." And with that, Walt Disney summarized his advice, *"Think, believe, dream, and dare."*

Going through life as kids we dreamed big. Our eyes got real wide and our faces lit up when we were asked the question: what do you want to be when you grow up? We might have said, "I want to go the moon" or "I want to build a colony on Mars" or "I want to be a doctor and save lives." As we get older, our enthusiasm fades. That twinkle is gone from our eyes. You ask someone who is thirty, forty, fifty years old, "What do you want to be when you grow up, what are your dreams?" They may reply, "Oh, I'm just doing it—same ole, same ole."

They settle and they compromise. Do we dream big as children? Yes. Do we dream big as adults? I don't know—it's questionable. Imagine if we all learned this most important lesson as young children. Do you think we would develop into brave, young adults without any self-limiting beliefs engraved in our subconscious? Definitely. So how do we become high achievers? By thinking we can. By dreaming. By envisioning. By doing.

Wright

This book, *Speaking of Success,* is a take-action type of book, so what actions do you anticipate readers will take after reading your part of the book?

Iurato

I believe that once they complete this book and absorb my chapter, they are going to sit down and reflect on their life—where they've been, where they are going, what they are doing. They will reevaluate their goals and their dreams. They are going to sit with their family, their spouses, their friends, their children, and they will have a goal-night or dream-night and share their feelings. They will put their dreams down on paper, talk about them, and share them with each other.

This new behavior will carry over in to their career. They will reevaluate where they are going in their career and in their life. I want them to ask and answer some very important questions: Are they really fulfilled with their life or are they just getting by? If they're not experiencing joy and fulfillment, they'll have to look at doing things differently to get closer to living their dreams. We all have dreams and desires, but most of them are in the back of our minds, they are not written down. We will soon forget the importance of our goals and dreams and as time passes, they disappear. Without meaning, our dreams lose their power; they lose momentum and run out of steam. Life then seems to pass us by. There's a good chance that we'll end up forty or fifty years old thinking, "Geeze where did it go? Twenty years, where has it gone?" So I believe this book will be a catalyst—it will be the driving force in getting people out of their comfort zones, taking risk, and being willing to fail so they can succeed. Daring to dream and discover new beginnings, a new life, a new spark. This will be the starting point of all of their achievements.

Wright

What's next for Brandon Iurato? What are your plans?

Iurato

There are a lot of people out there in the world looking for a spark—a fresh start. I get excited about sharing the tools and success strategies to get them on the path to their dreams.

Changing your life will take effort, new behaviors, new thinking. The majority of people don't want mediocrity, they don't want to be average, they don't want to go through life being a "C" player—they want to be an "A" player. In the game of life, do you want to watch—be a spectator? Or do you want to play—compete?

I have a book out now that will shed tremendous light on what we're talking about. This book will develop into a self-development series that people can use as their map—as their plan—not only to get closer to their dreams but to start living their dreams.

I will continue to conduct seminars and workshops throughout the country and share this message to forward thinkers who are willing to reinvent themselves and create the life they want.

So what's next? More books to help people, more seminars to reach people, and more interviews just like this.

Wright

You have said that you don't have any educational qualifications such as a PhD or an MBA for this type of book, so how have you gained your experience or knowledge?

Iurato

Most experts or authors won't admit they "lack" anything. Although I lack advanced degrees, I am highly educated. Working since I was eleven years old in dozens of jobs and in four careers, I've gained invaluable life experience and I have become a master at failing and overcoming obstacles. I apply what I have learned and what I am continually learning to my life, my family, and my business relationships. I take courses, attend seminars, and have an extensive library where I read and research every day.

I approach success in a no-nonsense manner. There are certain things that must be done in order to live your dreams. You have to do certain things in a certain way and I found that I have a unique talent in showing others how to do it. As a professional member of the National Speakers Association, a long-time member of Toastmasters and past President of my club, a member of the American Society of Training and Development, and participating in several coaching and sales organizations, I'm constantly and continually developing myself at a high level. I consider myself a lifelong student who has the ability to transfer specific knowledge to people looking for positive, lasting change. I enthusiastically encourage our readers to bravely walk their path to greatness.

Wright

What a great conversation, Brandon. I really do appreciate your taking this much time with me today to answer all these questions on success. I have learned a lot today and I'm sure our readers will.

Iurato

My thanks to you, David. The time was well spent and it is almost like therapy for me. When someone asks me these great questions, I get a lot out of it too, so thank you. I'd also like to thank the readers who are willing to take risks and pursue their dreams.

Wright

Today we have been talking with Brandon Iurato. He is founder and president of Success Strategies, a training development company that focuses on maximizing human potential. So what makes him so successful? As we have found here today, he has an uncommon commitment in the area of passion and enthusiasm and an unwavering positive mental attitude. He also has a sincere desire to help others on their path to success.

Brandon, thank you so much for being with us today on *Speaking of Success.*

About the Author

As founder and president of Success Strategies, Brandon Iurato likes to work with people who are interested in finding exciting ways to create results in life they are looking for. He lives in New York with his wife of twenty-one years, Jill. They enjoy spending time with their son Travis, riding their horses, taking walks with their dogs, and hiking the Appalachian Trail. Brandon's new book, *Mind Karate,* takes self-development to a new level. Brandon looks forward to hearing from you.

Brandon Iurato
Success Strategies
98 Eagle Crest Rd.
Port Jervis, New York 12771
Phone: 877.300.6226
E-mail: info@BrandonIurato.com
www.BrandonIurato.com

Chapter 15

JOHN BENTLEY

THE INTERVIEW

David Wright (Wright)

John Bentley is founder and President of Power 2 Transform. He brings more than twenty-five years of leadership and management experience to the organizations he serves. He honed his skills during a twenty-one-year military career where he personally built and led more than twenty-five teams throughout the United States, Canada, Europe, Central America, and Asia. His "nuts and bolts" ability to translate complex people issues into everyday practical business solutions resulted in numerous industry awards including the Chamber of Commerce Order of Merit Award and the Air Education and Training Command's Lance P. Sijan Leadership Award.

Through his speaking and training, John has helped over 5,000 people understand how clearly we communicate and how effectively we connect with people determine the outcome of our personal and professional lives. He excels in and enjoys helping people put together teams of significance and power and helping leaders move themselves and their staffs forward faster. Organizations large and small now benefit from his wealth of experience, which combines an understanding of human relations and business operations.

John, welcome to *Speaking of Success.*

John Bentley (Bentley)

Thank you, David, I'm glad to be here.

Wright

John, you've been in the success business for a number of years. How did you happen to focus your career on success strategies?

Bentley

Well, I believe the desire to help others is a natural human characteristic. The desire to help others achieve personal success or success in business simply branches from it. I realized the need and became involved in helping people achieve success during my first career in the military. My passion stems from my own experience on a fast track in the Air Force.

I was promoted to positions where I was responsible for producing results through others. But I discovered the approaches I used to accomplish my own work were not working for me as a team leader. In fact, my staff and I spent a lot of time finding fault and finger-pointing, which led to simply spinning our wheels, wasting resources, and delaying outcomes.

When I discovered and adopted behavior management, I began to communicate in a respectful way. This allowed us to see that our differences actually made us stronger, which led to a high level of trust. Our productivity soared and everyone wanted to be on our team.

Wright

You said that you "discovered" behavioral management as a tool. Was this concept new to you?

Bentley

Absolutely! The philosophy I learned from my father was this: don't trust other people to get things done; do everything yourself and strive for perfection. My father is a good person; his philosophy gave me a good work ethic and I carried his philosophy into my adult life and my Air Force career. This approach was very effective when I worked by myself, but caused difficulty once I reached a point where I needed to get things done through other people.

I'm going to fast-forward a little bit to 1992. I was disgusted with the Air Force. I wasn't getting promoted as fast as I thought I should. I decided to leave the Air Force because a $25,000 buyout was being offered to reduce the size of the military. I signed the paperwork knowing it meant the end of my career unless I received a promotion.

To my surprise, Chief Master Sergeant White pulled me aside and said, "John, if you were staying in the Air Force, I was going to move you into a new position and share with you an important life lesson. But since you are leaving, it's even more important that I share it now."

He shook the Coke bottle he was holding and handed it to me, and said, "John, I want you to open this."

Of course, I refused. He asked me why, and I replied, "Because it will spew all over me."

White responded, "John, that is exactly what you do when you're working with other people and things don't go your way. I want you to realize you can have all the talent in the world, but if you can't work with other people, you'll never succeed."

Three months later, I learned I was up for promotion. The promotion gave me a valid reason to stay in the Air Force. The main reason I changed my mind about leaving was Chief White showing me that my behavior was not helping me get to where I wanted to go; more importantly, I wasn't helping the Air Force succeed.

After deciding to continue my Air Force career, I looked for new philosophies and discovered a simple tool called "the iceberg model of human behavior." This model of human behavior provides a clear understanding of why people do what they do. It helped me discover why my beliefs were holding me back. (See Figure 1—Iceberg Model of Human Behavior.)

Using this model, the tip of the iceberg represents the behavior we display when interacting and relating with others. What's more important is to be able to go underneath the surface and look at our attitudes, our values, and our needs. If you really and truly want to function well with other people, you must go under the surface so you understand their values and their needs. Values and needs are the primary sources for an individual's motivation. Values-motivated behavior has to do with "why" a person does something and are standards of right and wrong, while needs-motivated behavior has to do with "how" a person acts. Basically, it has to do with what is natural and easy for one to do. For example, one person may prefer to work with people, while another person may prefer to work with tasks.

Fig. 1: Iceberg Model of Human Behavior

As I worked to understand people's needs, I was introduced to the DISC Behavior Model. It helped me understand "why people do what they do." The dimensions of Dominance, Influence, Steadiness, and Conscientiousness make up the model.

- **Dominance: Direct and Decisive:** strong-willed, strong-minded people who like accepting challenges, taking action, and getting immediate results.
- **Influence: Optimistic and Outgoing:** people-oriented and like participating on teams, sharing ideas, and energizing and entertaining others.
- **Steadiness: Sympathetic and Cooperative:** helpful people who like working behind the scenes, performing in consistent and predictable ways, and being good listeners.
- **Conscientiousness: Concerned and Correct:** sticklers for quality and like planning ahead, employing systematic approaches, and checking and rechecking for accuracy.

Becoming aware of behavioral styles was significant because it's the personal style that dictates the content of all verbal and non-verbal communications between people. One's message, whether it's to inform, explain, lead, manage, or convince, can only be communicated using one's own chosen behavioral style.

Your style is a powerful medium through which your beliefs and values, attitudes, education, skills, and everything about your life are conveyed to other people. Your behavioral style is also the source of disconnects with other people.

As we are in a life-long journey of understanding ourselves and building relationships, the question arises as to whether you can motivate other people. The answer is you can inspire them, encourage them, lead them, guide them, direct them, instruct them, threaten them, or put fear into them. But the power of true motivation lies only in each person.

Typical diversity programs focus only on our differences in race, age, and sex. These programs overlook the biggest difference in determining our success or failure in any endeavor—the whole person—represented by the iceberg model. Our behavior is what builds trust with others. When people trust one another they can solve problems. This leads to facilitating change, which ultimately satisfies the needs of the organization.

Wright

So, you learned a lot from your father in terms of approaching life differently than he did to be successful. Are there other people who influenced your growth after you started to explore success strategies?

Bentley

Looking back I was actually influenced by others even before I discovered their success strategy. My grandmother, for example, always found the good in other people. I never heard her say a bad word about anybody. She knew the way to get the best out of people was to focus on their strengths, not their weaknesses. This reminds me of the Andrew Carnegie quote that basically says you develop people the same way you mine gold. You've got to move tons of dirt before you find one little ounce of gold, but you don't go in looking for the dirt—you go in looking for the gold.

Then there's my mom. I am the oldest of her five children. My dad was a truck driver and he was usually home only on the weekends. It was my mother's perseverance I remember. She never gave up on anything worthwhile. She stuck with it and got it done.

John Cady was my supervisor when I was working in a restaurant. He taught me to become a student of every person I met because they all have something to share. We can choose whether it is a benefit to us and what to do with it.

Edwin Turbyfill taught me to give people the opportunity to grow and excel and to coach them when they make mistakes.

At one of the lowest points of my life, Dave Heuslein showed me a true friend is always with you and available to help no matter what the circumstances.

I already mentioned Russell White and his Coke bottle analogy. It taught me you can't lead sitting behind a desk and it is important to give feedback to others so they can learn and grow.

Two of my closest friends, Bill LeMaster and Kevin Rueter, with whom I've completed numerous projects in the Air Force, taught me none of us is as smart as all of us and you should always work from your strengths and allow others to do the same.

Dean Croiser taught me leaders care about their people and help them during difficult times in their lives.

I learned from Don Busbice you should live each day as if it were your last, and figure out what matters most and go for it.

Last, but not least, is my personal mentor, Anne Minton. She taught me relationships are what make our world of family, friendships, affiliations, teamwork, and businesses go around. Just as important, she helped me access, accept, and act on my God-given gifts, which led me to believing more in myself.

Wright

When did you start your own consulting firm, and what is the origin of the name: Power 2 Transform?

Bentley

Well, I started Power 2 Transform after I retired from the Air Force. I wanted to continue to deliver learning experiences that allowed people to enrich their lives and create winning work places. I describe "work place" as a family, an organization, a team, a church—basically anywhere we go to interact and relate with others. Through experience, research, and training, I expanded on the concept of personal behavior management to craft strategies creating successful organizations. When you discover and live your values while embracing change, you have the power to transform. The company name embodies my goal of working with individuals, teams, and organizations.

Wright

How do you see your past experiences contributing to the consulting services Power 2 Transform offers?

Bentley

The goal in any endeavor, no matter how large or small, is always to achieve a successful outcome. Everybody wants to succeed, but most don't know how to prepare for it. While in the Air Force, I worked for over twenty different leaders, each with different talents, personalities, backgrounds, lifestyles, religions, and prejudices. As you mentioned in the introduction, I built twenty-five teams around the world, so being successful meant knowing how to manage up, down, and across. I had the chance to learn about a large number of different personality types and discover the secret to helping them work together effectively. However, I think the most important insight my past experience has offered is the knowledge of how clearly we communicate and how effectively we connect with people determine the outcome of our personal success in all areas of our lives.

Wright

How would you describe the system you use for helping an individual team or organization to become successful?

Bentley

Having the opportunity to observe different individuals allowed me to develop a strategy I apply with my clients and myself. I learned it's not the smartest or the strongest who succeed, but those who adapt the most readily to changing environments.

Preparing for success isn't about stopping an organization to fix it. It's about equipping an organization's people with the ability to adapt to a changing environment while maintaining a focus on its purpose, goals, and guiding principles. Further, I approach each organization as a system. Organizations are made up of a number of systems, including strategies, structure, leadership, technology, and people. When a decision is made in any of these areas it affects every other area. If you don't lead people and manage organizations as a system, you won't achieve success.

Understanding and applying this principle helps my clients avoid worrying about keeping what they have or acting out of fear. It shifts the focus to improving individuals within an organization. This is an empowering approach that helps people in the organization improve and move forward faster. They have a strategy to follow that everyone can support because they can see how it will work and benefit everyone.

The strategy—the "5 Enablers of Success"—offers the ability to change, innovate, improve, reinvent, and renew using logic as opposed to acting out of fear, which inevitably drains one's ability to succeed. Most people just want to survive by not losing what they have. This philosophy will not motivate over the long haul. It offers no promise of forward motion, accomplishment, or improvement. The 5 Enablers of Success help organizations overcome assumptions that have always been in place regarding each other, customers, competition, and opportunities for growth.

Wright
What are the 5 Enablers of Success?

Bentley
The 5 Enablers are Vision, Skills, Motivation, Resources, and Execution Plan. (See Figure 2.)

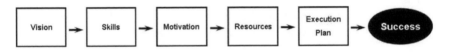

Fig. 2: 5 Enablers of Success

I would like to start with the first one—Vision—and then briefly discuss the last one—Execution Plan. I call these the enterprise-level management issues.

Vision is comprised of several components: a definition of an organization's purpose, why it exists beyond just making money; its guiding principles, commonly referred to as core values that define how the organization interacts internally and with customers to achieve the vision; and achievable stretch goals that link to individual and team objectives.

Of these, the most important to you and your organization are the guiding principles. Your guiding principles and purpose, when properly formed, should never change. Everything else—your business practices, goals, structures, systems, policies, and procedures—must be open for change because a constantly changing world demands it.

You may be wondering why you need to establish a vision in the first place. Why not let the organizations or teams operate by themselves and see what happens? That would work only if you really do not care whether the organization is successful or not.

By creating a vision, you provide a target to shoot for. All actions and efforts will be focused on achieving the vision. The Vision also provides employees with a sense of direction—a glimpse of where they're going. It provides a means to evaluate the organization's success and reward the people appropriately. It creates alignments, upholds an organization's guiding principles, and reinforces its purpose, which stimulates continuous improvement. If you don't shape your own future someone else surely will.

In fact, a recent study found that most companies have strategies, but 70–90 percent of them failed to execute those strategies. Execution is where organizations fall down most often. They fail to develop the second piece of this enterprise level, which is an execution plan.

In this step you create the road map to achieve your vision. It identifies short-term tactics and actions intended to move you and the organization in the direction of the long-term vision. It also identifies the groups responsible for implementing specific actions, a timetable for completion of these activities, a benchmark for monitoring progress, and other related information. The resulting execution plan is designed to be revised and updated several times over the lifetime of the Vision.

Wright

So, after the groundwork is laid at a management level, what comes next?

Bentley

The management level actually does lay the groundwork by involving the people in the process and creating a shared vision with common values. The next three enablers are skills, motivators, and resources, which gets down to the individual level and must be included in the execution plan.

Let's start with skills. When moving toward a vision, it's a given new skills will be required. Training is not new to small businesses or to large corporations. Employees must be trained to perform specific skill sets within their job functions and to follow global policies and procedures. This is especially true in today's constantly changing business environment.

It is imperative you provide adequate training and time to practice any new procedures. This is required to develop a new comfort level to replace the old. It usually takes about four weeks to develop a new habit, so training should be designed with this fact in mind. It's not effective to present a short seminar and expect someone to be confident after one or two sessions.

Invite your staff to tell you when they feel comfortable and confident with changes. This is important when training on new technical skills. But just as important, and probably more relevant, is the ability to work successfully with each other to solve problems and facilitate change.

Based on my experience I've learned that improving people skills will take you further than any technical or job improvement skill. So work to improve your ability to help people cope with change. Ask yourself: can you and your people work in teams to solve complex problems, and can you communicate clearly in print and in person? These skills are important to accomplish your organization's purpose and vision. Among the skills that will help workers are self-motivation, time management, strong oral and written communication, relationship building, problem-solving, information evaluation, and leadership.

In the future, even more emphasis will be placed on the skills that cannot be automated. These are termed hyper-human skills including caring, judgment, intuition, ethics, inspiration, friendliness, and imagination.

To achieve your Vision, you need the right skills, but just as important, you must understand why people do what they do—the motivators. Never forget that the greatest motivational tool is to be able to respond to the question, "What's in it for me?" For most individuals and most organizations motivation is about achievement, recognition, work itself, responsibility, advancement, and personal growth. So be sure the execution plan and communication addresses motivation opportunities for your people.

One way to do this is find out what individuals love to do and channel their work in this direction. Recognize an organization is a collection of individuals and address each person on his or her goals and desires. One thing to remember is you cannot motivate other people, but you can create an environment that allows each person to tap into their own personal motivation.

The DISC behavioral model is extremely helpful in this area. Challenge, power, and authority motivate the dominant behavioral style. The influential behavioral style is motivated by social recognition, group activities, and relationships. Stability and sincere appreciation motivate the steadiness behavioral style. Lastly, the conscientious behavioral style is motivated by clearly defined performance expectations, with quality and accuracy being valued.

When you approach each person based on his or her own motivational needs, you give each the ability to understand and connect in a way that makes sense to him or her. This creates buy-in and helps insure everyone is pulling in the same direction. Keeping the general workforce informed of what is happening, why it's happening, how it will affect them, and what will be expected is essential if conflict is to be minimized and resistance neutralized.

Now of course new skills and motivating factors are important, but without resources nothing gets done. I define resources as more than money, materials, and people. It also includes processes, policies, and systems. Here are the questions you must ask when developing an execution plan to insure you have the resources required to achieve your goals: Which of our people should take on each task? How much money will the project take? How much time will this take? How many people will it take? How much material will we need? What new skills will be required of our people? What new procedures, processes, or systems are required? These are simple questions, but they're not always easy to answer. Remember, people don't plan to fail—they fail to plan. More importantly, they don't take into account what is required at the individual level to insure your vision is achieved.

Wright

Will using the 5 Enablers work for any organization or team?

Bentley

Absolutely. Looking at Figure 3, you can determine why an organization may not be getting the results they want. We said earlier the 5 Enablers are Vision, Skills, Motivation, Resources, and Execution Plan. But what happens when one or more of these five enablers is missing?

Let's start with Vision. We know Vision sets the future direction for a company. If people are unaware of the Vision, there's a lot of uncertainty. People come to work wanting to do a good job and they are going to actively do something. If what they're doing doesn't support the Vision, you're burning up resources.

Now what happens when Skills are missing? I know when I was going to become a parent I didn't have any parenting skills. I had watched my mother, so I had seen those skills, but I didn't know if I could do them. It actually created a lot of apprehension for me. It works the same way with an organization. If you're bringing on a new software system, for example, your staff will be unsure of whether they'll be successful. They'll be afraid to fail and will experience a great deal of apprehension and anxiety.

Another result you may get is sporadic progress. In other words, if Motivation is missing, your employees don't know what's in it for them, or they don't feel like important contributors. Again, you're burning up resources and burning up dollars in labor costs; but people aren't actively engaged and progress toward the Vision is slowing down.

If Resources aren't there, but everything else is in place, there will be a lot of aggravation. And without the proper resources, it doesn't matter what else you have, you can't move forward.

Last, but not least, if we do not have an Execution Plan—the roadmap for accomplishment—there's disorder. Again, people will be moving in different directions, which leads to false starts. By using this as a diagnostic tool, you'll be able to see what may be missing and can jump on board with a solution to resolve the problems.

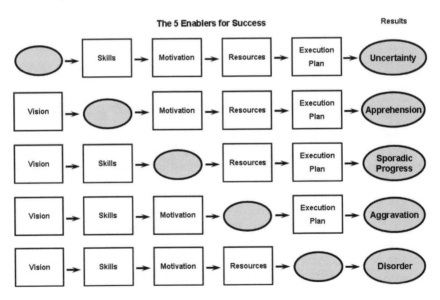

Fig. 3: 5 Enablers of Success Diagnostic Tool

Wright

After you start working with an organization, what do you find is the biggest challenge your clients face?

Bentley

The biggest challenge is waiting for the process to produce results. We all want immediate results. We live in an instant world and expect everything to happen now. We have instant pudding, microwave popcorn, and seven minutes to buns of steel, but there really are no silver bullets or magic formulas. What you need are realistic strategies for meeting your goals. I've learned there are no shortcuts to any place worth going.

Wright

What kind of results do you see when teams or companies successfully utilize the 5 Enablers of Success strategy?

Bentley

Leaders in one organization realized they had everything in place for future growth except skills. We conducted an assessment and discovered trust was an issue. Basically, the way they communicated with each other was causing stress and misunderstandings. We deployed our communication and trust process over seven months and provided individual coaching to ensure the learning worked. The reason for a process is one-day training events do not help change behavior. Behavior takes time to change so we structure our training accordingly and we get results.

The results were remarkable. We started with twenty-two people on their management team, but when we finished the process there were only sixteen left. Six people decided that they no longer wanted to work for the company because they would not buy into the CEO's long-term vision. As a result of the planning process, these six people realized that they either had to choose to change and change their behavior in terms of agreeing to operate by new guiding principles or leave. They left.

Now the organization is achieving more success with fewer people. Their conversations and hall talk are about the team members' strengths and contributions instead of what is wrong with them and how much they are disliked.

If I were to sum it up, the impact of the 5 Enablers of Success strategy on individuals, teams, or organizations would be this: It inspires leadership and innovation, not dependency; it fosters communication and teamwork, not control; it produces engaged employees, not compliant ones; it encourages change, not resistance to it, it creates a culture of trust, not suspicion; and it increases positive energy, not stress.

Wright

What advice do you have for managers who want to create winning workplaces?

Bentley

As leaders, you have a responsibility to recognize each individual's dignity as a human being and to learn to ask questions and help each of them remove obstacles. You do this by asking questions, listening more, and acting on what you learn for the betterment of the individual and ultimately the organization.

Building trusting and productive relationships is a part of the progression of life. Discovering your own personal strength, behavioral styles, internal motivators, and needs is your first step on the path. Awareness of these attributes and needs in others increases the possibility of effective communication and connection with your coworkers, team members, customers, family, and even with yourself.

My advice is to learn until the day you die because learning is a part of the reason for living. Good leaders allow themselves to question the status quo, assumptions, and the thinking used to generate solutions including their own. Good leaders are able to extract themselves from events and to view them objectively, even though they may have participated in or led the event. They understand what worked before may not be an appropriate solution this time.

Success in the workplace does not depend on the boss, owner, manager, leader, or employee. It is the willingness of the entire team to work toward a common goal while valuing the differences of each individual. You produce willingness by learning to manage yourself, manage relationships, and build trust. Only then can you develop others to their full potential and create an atmosphere where everyone can succeed.

Wright

It has been a pleasure speaking with you today.

Bentley

Thank you.

About the Author

JOHN BENTLEY is founder and President of Power 2 Transform, and brings more than twenty-five years of leadership and management experience to organizations he serves. He honed his skills during a twenty-one-year military career where he personally built and led more than twenty-five teams throughout the United States, Canada, Europe, Central America, and Asia. His "nuts and bolts" ability to translate complex people issues into everyday practical business solutions resulted in numerous industry awards: The Chamber of Commerce Order of Merit Award and the Air Education and Training Command's Lance P. Sijan Leadership Award.

Through his speaking and training, John has helped over 5,000 people understand that how clearly we communicate and how effectively we connect with people determine the outcome of our personal and professional lives. He excels in and enjoys helping people put together teams of significance and power and helping leaders move themselves and their staffs forward faster. Organizations large and small now benefit from his wealth of experience, which combines an understanding of human relations and business operations.

John Bentley
Power 2 Transform
1005 Ashworth St NE
Hartselle, AL 35640
Phone: 256.612.0015
E-mail: john@power2transform.com
www.power2transform.com